LIEB

Mike Figgis originally trained as a musician, and p——
an actor/musician with *The People Show* for fifteen years. He
directed his first film, *The House*, in 1984. Funded by
Channel 4, it was inspired by the work he had been doing with
his own theatre company. This film was followed by *Stormy
Monday* in 1987, and *Internal Affairs* in 1989.

LIEBESTRAUM

Mike Figgis

faber and faber
LONDON · BOSTON

First published in 1991
by Faber and Faber Limited
3 Queen Square London WC1N 3AU

Photoset by Wilmaset Birkenhead Wirral
Printed in England by Clays Ltd, St Ives plc

A CIP record for this book is available from the British Library

ISBN 0-571-16552-4

Contents

Introduction: Figgis on Figgis *edited by Walter Donohue*   ix

LIEBESTRAUM   I

Mike Figgis in Los Angeles

Introduction: Figgis on Figgis

WALTER DONOHUE: *You once said that* The People Show *was the best apprenticeship for film-making that you could think of.*

MIKE FIGGIS: I joined *The People Show* in 1970, having spent the year after I left college playing in France in a rock 'n' roll band, and deciding that I wasn't going to be a teacher, which is what I qualified to do. When I was a student I had moved to the Abbey Art Centre in London, which was where *The People Show* had been started in 1965 by Jeff Nuttall as a sort of 1960s version of a Happening. He called it *The People Show* because he collected seven people who happened to be there – drama students mainly – and put together a show, which he called *The People Show*. And afterwards, they just kept the name. They carried on for a few years doing his work, but eventually he drifted away, so they started doing their own scripts and working out their own structures.

And you just sort of drifted in.

Yeah. I was working with a free jazz group called The People Band, so named because they often worked with *The People Show*. I did a couple of shows at the old Arts Lab in Drury Lane as a musician and liked the work a lot. But, at a certain point, I got politically involved in the middle of a huge dispute between the musicians and the actors. The musicians felt that they weren't being given enough room to be truly improvisatory and were being held back by what they felt were the too rigid structures of the performance element of the show. I felt that if you elected to be in that situation, there were certain rules you should obey, otherwise the anarchic element would ultimately destroy what was good about the combination. There was a huge fight one night, a split occurred, and The People Band walked out. I felt very strongly that they were wrong, so I stayed. I then joined *The People Show* as its musician.

But you weren't content simply to be a musician. You wanted to be involved in a much broader way, didn't you?

Because *The People Show* was the kind of group that never had a director – never had a production designer – everybody did everything. You were expected to cross over into every area. So, although I was mainly there to do the sound, I also very quickly became a performer. I remember my first performance was at the Come Together Festival at the Royal Court Theatre in 1970 in front of a very hip, very aware audience. It was terrifying. I had to wear a dress. Both Mark Long and I wore the same dress. The show was about Bix Beiderbecke and Mark Long's mother. Within ten minutes of the show starting, it went very well. It was very funny, and short enough so we didn't get into trouble. I didn't look back after that. Because it worked, no one really then questioned the idea of whether you were a performer or not, whether you could act or not. You just carried on.

Did being a performer also mean writing your own material?
Each performer in *The People Show* was responsible for his own lines, so I became very actively involved in the writing of the scripts.

Writing meant what? Writing speeches?
No speeches were ever written. Our method was, basically, locking the door and the three or four performers sitting together and not coming out of the room – other than to sleep – until you had unanimously decided that the structure was correct. It meant hours and hours of talking about structure. Someone would suggest an image at the beginning of the process. Someone would say: I have this image. And it would usually be a painterly image. It would be: broken glass or a rose. In fact, they sound rather bland. Usually, it would be a strange image. There would be a surreal quality to the image. But it would be an image in isolation. This image would trigger off other images, and then one would find a connecting image, and so on. Then, through a natural process of selection, certain images would be put on the shelf, perhaps for another show. Everyone kept notebooks. So, the whole notion of a notebook became crucial as a reference for this process of work. Then, having assembled a certain number of images, the hard work of actually connecting those images and coming up with a dramatic structure – which was a sort of storyline, which would also involve characters – would begin. Maybe, one of the images suggested in the first place would literally be a character. Mark Long would say: I want to do this in a red face, and I'm going to wear these clothes. That's my character. And my obsession is cleaning windows. Now, that might change as we talked, but the red face would probably remain, and he'd have this very strong sense of character. With Mark, it was always a very strong sense of character.

And with you?
With me, it was more an overall sense of how 'red face' and 'broken glass' could connect. I became the main notebook writer; in a sense, the person who co-ordinated the images. Not exclusively. Everyone did it. But by the time I left *The People Show*, a situation had naturally evolved whereby on the last day of the meeting I would come in and say: OK, here's the order. Because I was the person who made the sound tapes, the timings of which would be used as triggers for certain light cues, and the appearances or disappearances of characters – these sound timings providing the skeleton of the show – it seemed natural to be the one who came in and said: OK, here's the order. Mark and I would then work closely together to get the lights cued up. And of course Mark, as a performer, was very much in the front. So his sense of character was very important. My sense of character always evolved much more slowly, as a result of the performances. I would tend to, in the more successful shows, write myself as a kind of watching character who would just stand at a bar and drink, and then do small things, and have an overall view. In a sense, like a director.

This idea of having images be the starting point – in terms of the films which you have written yourself, has this been the process?
No. The starting point tends to be ideas, not visual images.

So, the image of the couple sprawled on the floor at the end of Liebestraum *was not the starting point of the film.*
No. But when I look at the stills from *Liebestraum*, I suddenly realize exactly what they are: they're images from *People Shows*. The image of the couple on the floor at the end is an image from a performance I did in a basement. I was still with *The People Show*, but it was one of the first things I did on my own. There's a striking similarity. And there are other images in *Liebestraum*. There's one from *Redheugh*. It was an image to do with earth, with being buried in earth.

Where does that occur in Liebestraum?
It's the image of the store covered in dirt. Also, the image at the end: the couple lying in dirt, lying in soil, ambiguously dead or alive. These images tend to recur.

Like in The House: *the soldier lying, covered in snow. You're not sure whether he's dead or alive.*

Also, the lovers in *The House*, lying in the room covered in cobwebs.

So, for a number of years you worked with The People Show.
I was with *The People Show* for ten years, but then the group started to change. The advent of what was called *The Cabaret Show* took *The People Show* in a whole new direction. It was a bit more commercial, very funny, very entertaining, but much less surreal, much less confrontational. The situation on the fringe was changing. It was hard to get grants, venues were closing, and, in a sense, one had to adapt. I have to say, with complete admiration, that *The People Show* still exists, and that is probably because of their ability to adapt. I had ambitions that we could adapt in a different way. So, I decided that probably the best thing for me to do was to stand back and do something else for a while, and by then I'd become very interested in film.

The National Film School had opened a few years before, it sounded like a really good place, so I applied to go there. I read the prospectus and it seemed that, in a sense, I was their most perfect student. I'd done everything they wanted one of their students to have done, i.e. I was between the age of twenty-five and thirty-five, and I'd had a wide experience of a number of film-related things: lighting, acting, directing, writing, music, etc. So, I assumed I'd get in. I probably even told people that's what I was going to be doing for the next couple of years. But when I went for the interview it went very badly.

Why?
I think because I assumed I'd get in, and they probably picked this up as a form of arrogance. Coupled with this, I think, was their natural suspicion of theatre, particularly experimental theatre. You know, the idea that you can't cross over, that there is not a strong connection between the two, and that it's an arrogant assumption to think that there is. David Putnam was on the panel, as well as Colin Young. Romaine Hart was very sympathetic. There were also a couple of well-established television and film people. I found them very hostile, and I then in turn became aggressive. In all honesty, I was surprised at their attitude, which was: You've had no experience in film, so what makes you think you'd be any good at it? I said: Well, I think it's self-explanatory. The work that I've done is so closely related to film that I don't see that it's going to be a huge leap.

The only thing I don't know is camera technique. I made the mistake of saying 'and it can't be that difficult'.

The National Film School tends to be seen as an avenue to get people into the industry, so probably what they're looking for is people who can fit into the industry.
I think so. They kept using the expression 'teamwork', that film-making is essentially a team process and that I didn't seem to be expressing a team attitude. Yes, of course, you can't make a film without a team, but I don't actually think it is a team process. I think it's a singular vision. And I think that probably worried them a little bit.

In a way, the perfect product of the Film School is Michael Caton Jones. There isn't a single vision in any of his films.
I was very surprised. It was literally my first experience with film people, and in a sense it was a very accurate taste of, certainly, the British attitude to film-making.

Which is?
The old boy network. You have to pay your dues. It's not a thing you can jump into and be clever with very quickly. It's something you have to swim through mud to get to the point where they'll give you the toys.
   I mean, everyone said: Keep your mouth shut. You can do it if you keep your mouth shut. Your credits are sound credits, so say you want to be a sound recordist, and then you can change once you've got it. But it seemed to incense the panel that I wanted to do directing, and also camera. They said: Why do you want to do both? And I said: If you don't understand camera, how can you direct a film? So, to cut a long story short, the application was rejected. Putnum said: If you don't get in, what are you going to do? And I said: I'll make a film anyway. He said: But you've already said that you can't use a camera. And I said: Yes, and I've already said that it can't be that difficult. I'll work it out. So, I decided that that would be my goal. I'd make a film. Which I then did.

Which was?
Redheugh.

I thought that was a theatre piece?
I'd written a film script which was basically a forty-minute film about the war. My father had died a couple of years before. He'd been a pilot in World War Two, and it had been my

observation that he – and most of his generation – had never recovered from the war, emotionally recovered. Anyone who was seventeen or eighteen when the war started and was therefore twenty-four or twenty-five when it finished – those crucial years when you're gently meant to be growing up – if you grow up in three weeks in a war situation and then spend the next couple of years – as my father did – drinking heavily to get over your fear of flying, when the war finishes, what are you fit for? You've missed out on a whole psychological period, and he spent the rest of his life trying to deal with it. So, I wanted to make a little film about a pilot who gets shot down in the north of England. But then, to make it ambiguous, it could have been in Germany or England, he could have been dead or alive. There was very much a kind of 'is this really happening' feel to the piece.

I obviously wasn't going to get the money to make it as a pure film, so I formed a theatre company, with myself as the director. I got a writer's grant from the Arts Council, and then wrote to the Mickery Theatre in Amsterdam to Ritsaert Ten Cate, who'd been a firm supporter of *The People Show*, told him I was writing my own first piece, and would he be interested in it. He said he would. Ultimately, they came in as the main producers with the ICA, and he put up £6000 to make the film – which was very brave of him. I then went ahead and made the film up in Northumberland at the house where my father had died. I brought the material back to London, edited it, and ended up with a forty-minute film which then became the central part of a live performance involving four classical musicians, an opera singer, three other actors, and a fairly complicated technical set. But the film was the starting point for the performance; in other words, the live performance elements all came from elements within the film. The film also functioned by itself as a film.

This also coincided with the beginning of Channel Four. I was aware of the fact that Channel Four was opening. Very quickly word got round that Channel Four was commissioning films, and that they were interested in people who had not been in the industry before, and that they were going to help new people. I had my *Redheugh* film, as well as added pages of script that had originally been taken care of in the live performance. So, my proposition was: Here is half a film. With very little money we could complete the film, add a score, and so on, and you'd have a complete film. That was really the extent of my ambition.

I remember coming to the meeting at Channel Four and there was David Rose, and yourself, and probably Karin Bamborough, and pitching this very complicated, rather experimental idea, and leaving a video cassette of the film, as well as a sound cassette of the songs that had been written for the film. I came back for the second meeting and you, I think, said: Look, I don't think this is going to be so interesting for us. It's something you've already done. We'd be much more interested in commissioning something completely original, written especially for the Channel, not something that's half-done and then adapted. So, I was suddenly in one of those situations in which you occasionally find yourself, where someone says: Do you have anything else? In fact, this is where the notebook pays off. If you do keep a notebook, then of course, you always have things half-cooking. And I did have one idea which had been commissioned, but hadn't, in fact, materialized. It was for a festival in Paris. The idea was that six different performance artists were each going to be given a house in which to make a performance. The piece had to be about a house. I had come up with the idea of a house which was an English house, but it wasn't in England, it was in the middle of Europe. So, the whole philosophy and approach would be different; the idea of the English being an island race would be challenged by putting them in a different environment. I already had a map with England in the middle of Europe, which was a striking visual image. I then handed this over, saying: Yeah, I have an idea. David Rose immediately picked up on it and said: That's an interesting idea. Yes. I think we can talk about this. So, between you and David, it got kicked off. The next stage was the crucial one: who was going to write it? I remember being very nervous about that and suggesting to you that Jeff Nuttall be brought in since he was a writer I knew. What's interesting is that I was intimidated, in the sense that because it was a film, it had to have a more conventional approach to it. There should be lots of words on a page. And you said: Well, why don't you write it? I said: No, I can't write it. And you said: Well, why don't you just do the first draft. If it's terrible, we can then talk about what writers we could bring in. In fact, when I brought in the first draft, from then on in, the conversations were solely about the script, not about bringing in a writer. I'm sure everyone goes through that paranoia about whether they can write or not. Film writing is such a different thing from theatre writing.

Different in what way?
It's a much more minimal thing. You have far more tools to play with in a film, such as the visual elements, and all the other things that come in post-production which make a film work and which aren't actually the script or the dialogue as a dominant thing above everything else. I mean, you need dialogue. But if you choose your actors well, they're usually pretty good at dialogue. If you give them an indication of what you want, give them dialogue as a guide, and work with them in an interesting way, they'll come up with their own speech patterns which are more authentic anyway than anything you could try to write for them. There are areas where things have to be said briefly and they're usually to do with plot and you don't really want to spend more time on that than you need to. You should write those in as precise a way as possible and stick to that. But writing is not nearly as intimidating a thing as I thought it would be. And the transition from thinking of oneself as not being capable of doing that to suddenly accepting that you are a writer of films was, in this particular instance, totally painless.

In a sense the film was more like your theatre pieces. It didn't have a conventional narrative in any way. It was much more poetic.
Yes. As a transition from theatre to film, it was perfect because I was allowed to work in a theatrical way. There was a lot of voice-over. The main dialogue in the film is Stephen Rea's voice-over as he is dying in the snow.

And what is the film about?
It's about trying to return to one's home. In this particular case, it's an England which is set in the middle of Europe, with Stephen Rea as an English soldier who is returning from a failed campaign in which the English army have tried to invade the neighbouring state of Latvia.

For what reason?
For reasons of late nineteenth-century imperialism. In fact, in the story, Russia has stepped in and signed an alliance with Latvia, using it as an excuse to counter-invade England. So, it's New Year's Eve and a party is taking place in a country house. There's a bishop there, and a general, and a rather degenerate aristocrat whose house it is, and his very young wife who is

grieving over the death of their child in an accident when the child fell down the stairs. They're all talking about the rumours of whether the Russians are coming.

At the beginning of the film you see a soldier, the Stephen Rea character, who is the main character of the film, and who is in the house as a ghost, but we also see him walking through the snow in a blizzard. He collapses and is so tired that he decides just to die in the snow. So, the voice-over that goes through the entire film is his thoughts, his recollections of the campaign in Latvia – where he has just been – of this house, and of the affair that he had with the woman in the house. He struggles for a while in the snow, and then just lies there. And the camera then tilts up over the next hill and you see that he's only about a quarter of a mile from the house, but he can't see it. The camera then zooms in on the house, and then the interior stuff of the film begins and we go into the party. In the course of the one hour that the film takes, the house ages and begins to fall apart and get tattier. Similarly, as the party progresses, they get more and more drunk, and they end up in the opium room completely out of it as the Russian soldiers come in – along with the Communist elements of the English army who have revolted – and start burning and looting the house.

EUROPE 1884

The soldier is a ghost in the house, but he also has recollections of the house he was billeted in in Latvia when he was part of the conquering army. Isn't there a danger that having these different levels of reality could lead to confusion in the audience?

Well, it goes back to *The People Show*, and a mentality where the ability to juggle a lot of ideas at the same time is highly developed and seems like a natural thing. It's certainly characteristic of the French films that came out in the 1960s and 70s, like *Hiroshima Mon Amour*, *Last Year at Marienbad*, *Providence*, and, in a different way, the work of Jean-Luc Godard. So, with something like *The House*, which in the space of an hour certainly presents a lot of very complicated ideas in conflict and in parallel with one another, I spent very little time worrying about whether the audience would understand it or not. I just spent all my time trying to make it as seamless as possible as a piece of work so that even if they didn't consciously understand it, at least their sub-conscious would click in and people would start to understand it at that level. So, what is dictated to by their ego – which is the need to apparently understand something, which often confuses and gets in the way of the way people look at art – can be over-ridden by a kind of sophisticated style. I believe that if someone is enjoying something, and is taken on a journey by something, then they will let go.

One of the strongest moments in *The House* was when the soldier and the young wife make love in the abandoned nursery. From her point of view, the sexual element is very much a grieving; for him, it coincides with this story he is telling as a dying soldier about an affair he had with a woman in the occupied town he was in, which then becomes part of a story about walking down a hill behind an old man and having the urge to kill him – just experiencing the sense of power of being a conquering soldier and how that destroyed him, having to confront the fact that it existed in himself as a human being. All this coincides with him walking down the stairs behind the young wife who is going down to rejoin her husband, and the camera does this incredible move right round in a circle and comes back up on to the soldier who is watching. Meanwhile, his voice-over is telling a different story, which builds up to a point where he suddenly sees the ghost of the child. He's talking about death, and the child suddenly appears and throws himself down the stairs and kills himself, in a flashback, at the soldier's feet. Now, if you had asked someone who had watched this to explain it, he probably couldn't have. But because all those different elements coincided at that time, there was a very strong emotional impact.

When you make your first film – and I think I have this in common with every film-maker – you think you might never make another film. So, you cram so much into it. In *The House*, in the space of one hour, I had so many ideas and images going through it. It's only when you get a little bit more secure, as you carry on working, that you realize that you don't need to put every single idea in your head into the film you're making at the time. You can have fewer ideas and expand them more.

So, what happened next?
I got into a commission situation with Enigma. Putnam had seen a preview of *The House*, and I got a call from his producer, Susan Richards, who said: David and I have seen *The House* and we're terribly excited. We're looking for new film-makers, so come and have a drink with us. It was all very nice and exactly the way one would always like it to be.

Did you remind David Putnam about your previous encounter with him?
No. He claimed never to have met me before, and I didn't argue with him. I'd learned something. They were ecstatic about my idea. I had written a short film called *Mindless Violence*, about a gangland execution which took place in Newcastle right underneath the bridges I used in *Stormy Monday*. I had sent it to the BFI, trying to get it made as a short film, but it was rejected. They found it visually stimulating, but politically vacuous – I think that's what the letter said. It was a long tracking shot down a hill as a man was taken to be executed. So, I had this idea of a gangland thriller in Newcastle. I pitched that, and they loved it and said: Do that for us. Don't talk to anyone else about it. We'll definitely make this film. So, that was great. I went away with the idea that I was going to make this feature film. And then nothing happened. I ended up teaching again at Middlesex Poly in their film course, and also keeping my theatre work going. I started another piece called *Animals of the City*, elements of which ended up in *Liebestraum*: a lot to do with architecture, cast-iron buildings, and things like that. So, I waited, and nothing happened. I never heard back from David Putnam. I don't think he even read the treatment. Susan Richards would say: I think you need to do more work on the treatment, and I kept

saying: You can do treatments forever. It's not until you actually try and write a script that you start to understand what your problems are. Just commission a script. But they didn't.

So, how did Stormy Monday *get made?*
I was in Soho one day in my car in a little connecting street between Wardour Street and Dean Street, and I saw a skip full of sound tapes. I was working at the Polytechnic, and they were running out of money, and I looked in the skip and there were maybe a thousand five-inch reels of tape being thrown out. They'd been used maybe once. I thought this was criminal. So, I opened the boot of the car and was unloading all this stuff out of the skip when Nigel Stafford-Clark, who had produced *The House*, walked past. He asked me how it was going. And I said: Not very well, as you can see. I think Nigel was a bit embarrassed to be having a conversation with a person who was obviously unloading a skip, so I stepped out of the skip, we walked to the other side of the street, and I told him what had happened. He said: Well, let me see the treatment. So, I got him the treatment the next day. And within a day – all credit to Nigel – he rang me back and said: Look, I have three or four points about your treatment. I think it's too complicated, but basically I think it's a good idea and if you're prepared to take on board my suggestions, I'll commission a script. He then went to Channel Four and got it as a Film on Four, for part of the finance. On the strength of that, he took it to British Screen and got well over half the finance for the film, which was budgeted at 1.3 million pounds. So, we still needed to raise just under half of the money. But on the strength of that, he got the script commissioned. It went through its first and second drafts, and then it was really just a question of getting the finance from the Americans. Simon Relph was consistently supportive from the very beginning, even at a time when the finance fell through in America.

Was the presence of American characters in Stormy Monday *done primarily to raise the American finance?*
No, I wanted that. I think the best parallel would be a musical one. If I'd been writing a piece of music and someone said you can have whoever you like to play on this, I would have brought in some American musicians. I think American actors are better film actors by and large, and certainly having the spice of some American actors in a British film, particularly a film set outside London, in a place like Newcastle which I knew was gritty and

had a kind of American quality anyway, was something I found very attractive.

The whole point of the film was the Americanization of our culture. The willing take-over. We certainly haven't fought the Americans, or tried keeping them out. I think it's because we always wanted that in our culture. It was an exciting infusion into British music, and certainly into film. I've never felt that I was an English artist, anyway. So, purely from the point of view of: you can have whoever you'd like to work with in the film – Melanie Griffith would have come pretty near the top of my list.

What's interesting about your films is the level of acting in them. Sting, Richard Gere, Kim Novak have never given better performances. In Stormy Monday *you had Hollywood stars, rock stars, fringe-theatre actors, as well as a wide range of actors with different degrees of film experience. Yet all of them appear to be seamlessly a part of the same world. How do you achieve performances which are so natural?*
When you start to direct a film – I mean literally directing it – I think you have to let your unconscious instincts dictate a lot of what you are doing. One of the first things is that you have to be so aware of people's nervousness and their ability – and the combination of these things – that you can decide how to apportion your time, in terms of who you are going to help. Obviously, the more people there are in a scene, the more difficult that becomes. Like with Sting. He's a nice man; he's not at all a confrontational, aggressive man. There's a scene in the film where Sean Bean turns up at his house to warn him about a plot against him. This was the first scene Sting shot. He's sitting at the breakfast table. I let him do the scene, but basically what he did was, he decided he needed cigarettes as a prop. So, he took a cigarette out, put it in his mouth, offered them to Sean Bean, who declined, then he lit the cigarette, and tapped it on the table. There was a lot of this kind of little finger acting going on. So, after we rehearsed it for a while, I had a cup of coffee with him and said: Look, there's a couple of things I want to say, and I hope you won't be offended, but you're being very busy with your hands, and I think that if you just kept very, very still it would be much stronger. Do you mind me saying this? And he said: No, no. I can't tell you how grateful I am for someone telling me how to act. I'm comfortable acting, but I have no sense of what I'm doing with

my body. And if you could tell me that, I would be very grateful.

Other actors, however, when you start to pick on mannerisms and things like that, would be fearfully offended and feel that somehow you were attacking their performance. More trained actors, of course, study themselves in the mirror, and those little mannerisms are crucial.

How do you find a way of maximizing an actor's good points and minimizing the weaknesses they have?
Well, you watch, of course. It really goes back to *The People Show* and the whole idea that most of the creative work comes from notes, rather than literally from rehearsals: you do the rehearsal and then just use that as a basis for talking. My big thing when I'm shooting is that I don't allow anyone to make any noise for the two minutes immediately following a shot. The only time I would ever be angry or lose my temper was if people abused that. You forget very, very quickly the details. So, I like to come in immediately after a rehearsal or a take and say: OK, that hand movement didn't work, hold the hand down, don't look up, say the line, just keep looking down – moving very quickly. It then may take half an hour before we can do the shot again because things have to be adapted, but I want to get my notes in straightaway.

So, that's one thing. The second thing, I think, is creating an atmosphere on the set, participating to such an extent with enthusiasm and with your spirit that you never dissociate yourself. The minute you dissociate yourself from what's going on, the actors become insecure. If you're in there making a fool of yourself as much as you're asking them to, then they'll go along with you. If it's working well, you'll end up with such an atmosphere on the set that even the less able actors will give something and be natural.

A lot of Stormy Monday *takes place at night. Was that a problem?*
The start date got delayed and delayed and delayed. So, we ended up shooting bang on mid-summer in the north of England where night starts – in real dark terms – about 11 o'clock at night, and dawn begins at about 4 or 4.30. So, you might have five hours maximum to shoot a whole night scene. You'd start shooting a scene, and you'd be doing one angle, and you'd suddenly realize that you weren't going to be able to turn around because it was going to be dawn. There'd be this dreadful moment when the birds would start to sing and you'd know that that was it. Those things were very frustrating. In fact, one of the best things in the film was shot after one of the worst nights of the film. The scene when Tommy Lee Jones and Sting are walking across the bridge at the crack of dawn, we grabbed that on the run after a night of filming, in the rain, the final scene outside the nightclub. All communication had broken down, everyone was in a bad temper, nothing worked – it was just desperate.

In that end scene Melanie Griffith and Sean Bean disappear up the steps and Sting is the last character you see. Somehow you miss a final moment between the two lovers.
I think so. I remember when I was cutting it, longing for that last moment. It was a very strong lesson in how important an ending is, the last image you leave everyone with. I felt it was weak. I felt I would have liked to have stayed with our lovers, and had that extra moment.

Well, you said that was the worst night of the shoot.
It was. And there is that awful reality when you make films, that the budget is a real thing, the schedule is a real thing, and you have to make the best of what you have in the cutting room afterwards. So, you find yourself using every trick, every artistic device you can engender, to make the film flow to the end in

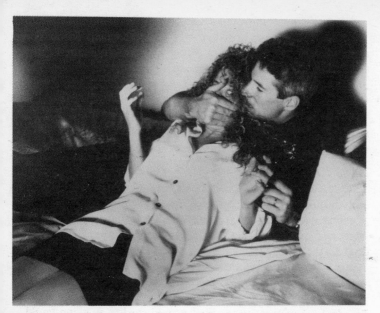

such a way that you minimize the fact that the ending was a
little inadequate for the emotion that had been set up just prior
to the ending. If I'd have had the power to do it, I would have
got back on to the streets with a camera, got Melanie Griffith
and Sean Bean back, and shot another scene the way Woody
Allen is able to. But the reality is, you can't do that. Not only
can you not do that, they start saying: And you've only got
another two weeks left to edit. It's got to finish. I mean, this is a
budget of 1.5 million pounds. It doesn't buy you anything.

Yet, in your next film, Internal Affairs, *the final image is right.
Richard Gere is lying dead on the floor, and Andy Garcia goes over
to Nancy Travis and puts his arms around her, thereby resolving the
conflict that had erupted between them, largely through the
instigation of Richard Gere.*
Yes, but that was a re-shoot.

The last image?
No. The whole last scene was re-shot. As a result of a preview
audience, it was felt that the original ending left the audience
very dissatisfied. The original ending had Richard Gere coming
into the apartment, terrorizing the wife in a much more bizarre
way, too. His foot had a bullet in it and he made her take his
shoe off and start to clean his foot. He's suddenly very
ambiguous with her, in the way he's talking to her almost in a

sexual way as she's tending his foot. It was very perverse. Then Andy walks in totally unprepared, walks straight into a trap, and Richard Gere shoots him. Almost kills him. As Richard is about to kill the wife, Andy gets up, makes a superhuman effort, runs at Richard, and they both crash through the window and fall through the air into the swimming pool. Richard tries to drown Andy, but at the last moment Andy manages to get his gun out and kills Richard, but in doing so he almost dies himself. You think they're both dead. The wife then jumps into the water and drags Andy on to the side of the pool, tries to revive him, hits him, slaps him, and eventually he wakes up and vomits. As he does so, Richard Gere bobs to the surface right next to them. It was wonderful. The audience were so frightened. They thought Richard was going to get out of the pool. But, this ending was felt to be unsatisfying because Andy had not played the role of the avenger and coldly executed Richard like a mad dog. Personally, I liked the fact that Andy wasn't a hero, that the line between the two of them was very marginal, and that he had almost died. I also liked the fact that it was the woman who had the strength to revive him and to demonstrate how much she cared by reviving him. She was actually shouting at him: Don't die! as she was hitting him. And when he revived, she started laughing, and they lay there together, next to the pool, and the camera very, very slowly went up and you saw Richard floating in the pool, and the two of them, and you could hear the ambulance coming.

And the film was a commercial success.
Yes. The commercial success of the film was helped by the re-shoot because the audience was able to come out in some way resolved. To be fair, I think the ending is a very cold ending, which I like. There's nothing warm or heroic about the way Andy does it. He's very cold. I think he suddenly walked straight into the *Godfather* part in that last scene.

One of the achievements of the film is how it revived Richard Gere's career. Why is he so good in the film?
I think he's a really good actor. He's not a 'regular' actor. A regular actor is someone who, regardless of how they feel, will turn in a good performance, and you never really get that much of a glimpse into their soul. I think Richard's performances, good and bad, have always been characterized by his personality. And I think that's what sets him apart from most of his contemporaries. He is that breed of actor, whether you like

him or not, that has a certain special quality, which is his personality. And you are aware that there is a complex personality at work. If you get an actor like Richard who is on a break in his career where he's had a huge high and then a trough, where he's done three or four films that haven't come off, you're getting him at a point where he's very open and vulnerable, and he's going to push. The Dennis Peck character is a very complex part, and the other actors I spoke to wanted to play it as the macho man, wanted to play it as a kind of psycho comedy, which horrified me because I think it's pornographic. Richard was the only one who was prepared to look at it for what it really was: a complicated, psychological, ultimately sympathetic part. And if you were prepared to be bold with it, it would be very interesting.

I think one of the best scenes in the film is the aftermath of Gere killing William Baldwin and how Gere deals with the complexity of emotions generated by that action.

It was a very interesting night's work. We were shooting in east Los Angeles, which is very dangerous. There were drive-by shootings going on as we shot. You could hear automatic gun-fire all night. It was a very spooky place, an absolutely perfect environment in one sense.

There was a very slow build-up. We had to do the stunt first – William Baldwin being shot – which was horrific. And then all the stuff with the guns. And then the scene itself – which was shot in one take with two cameras – and very, very slowly stoking Richard up. The scene was basically Richard because William Baldwin is dying, so his part was simple. William Baldwin did it very well; he's very good at taking direction. But Richard had the major acting to do. So we'd do a rehearsal, or a take, and I'd go straight to Richard, and we'd go into a huddle, and it never stopped: You've got that, and that, now push that look even more, push the feeling of 'what the fuck am I going to do', that's your key thing. And then we'd go straightaway again. It was quite an extraordinary night. From my point of view it was one of the best directing nights I've ever had just because you were aware of an actor's clicking into a role in an extraordinary way.

And then there was an accident which almost stopped the whole evening. The effects man gave us the weapon Richard was to use when he was shooting the guy he had hired to shoot William Baldwin. He had to shoot him through the head, and I wanted to get the image, that Vietnam image of the man being shot in the street. We had a technical problem which was that Richard had to shoot him, but the camera was in profile so you've either got to see a flash or you've got to put the camera in such a way that you can't see the muzzle of the gun. We obviously couldn't have a flash because it was right next to the stunt man's head. I was just trying to deal with this problem technically, so I said: OK, since we're not going to use a charge in the gun, if Richard puts the gun to his temple so that the muzzle's hidden with his hair, is that going to be all right? And the effects man said: That'll be fine, don't worry about it. So, we rehearsed it, and in the rehearsal the stunt man wanted to act, he wanted to do a huge death and throw his arms up, and I said: No. If someone shoots you through the head, my theory is that you'll just drop like a stone. You won't have time to react. There might be a twitch, but you have to just go straight down. So we went for a full rehearsal and Richard put the gun to his head, pulled the trigger – no charge in it, of course – the guy made a huge movement with his arms, and fell to the ground. I said: Cut! and was very angry. I said: No, no, don't move your arms like that. And I looked down and the guy wasn't moving, he was just lying on the ground. And I said: Are you all right? He started to move very slowly and he had blood on his head. What had happened was that the gun we were using had a recoil

action. You fire the bullet, and the barrel shoots forward and ejects the empty cartridge shell. So Richard had put the gun hard on this man's temple, and like a jack-hammer, the barrel had smacked into his temple and knocked him to the ground.

Richard is a Buddhist and he said to the effects man: Why did this happen? Why did you tell me it was all right? The effects man apologized and tried to bluff his way out of it, but Richard said: Look, I can't deal with this. And he walked off and went to his caravan and wouldn't come back on the set because he was so upset that he had almost killed this man that he was pretending to kill. You can deal with one reality as an actor, but not two.

How did you get Richard back on the set?
I went and talked to him and said that we had to deal with it, and apologized for the mistake. It was the last thing I wanted to happen, but we had to get over it. I was pretty shaken. There we were in this very violent street, with these gunshots going off, pretending to do something, which almost really hurt someone. The morality of what you're doing suddenly hits you in a different way. It's hard to deal with these emotions at the same time as keeping this fantasy going.

These are the things which they can't teach you in film school. In a situation like that there's only one person who can keep the thing going, only one person who can get the actor back on the set. So, how did you find the language to do that? No matter what you're feeling at the moment, you know that, on the other hand, you've got to carry on.
It's very hard. Again, it's like the directing thing. You have to make the judgement based entirely on who it is. Sometimes you actually have to shout at people, which might be totally against your nature. Sometimes you have to publicly shout at someone to let them know, on a purely animalistic level, that you can shout and be as angry and as aggressive as they appear to be. It's the only way to get it to move. Other times you mustn't do that. You must be very gentle, and almost gently put it back on to them.

What I said to Richard was: If you don't want to come back, I understand and I agree with you. And if that's how you feel, I'll back you on that because I feel this is an unforgiveable incident and you're perfectly within your rights to withdraw your acting services, because you are giving everything and you were not protected. And Richard said: Just give me twenty minutes and I'll be OK. I just need some time by myself now. As a result of all this, when Richard did the scene he was extraordinary. I'm a believer in the primitive gestures that people make. And this one where you cover your face with your hands is one of the strongest gestures in terms of body language that we have. I suggested to Richard that he use his hands in that way, and the point where he decides to do that is incredibly strong. He just covers his face, and there is a moment when his head goes down and his shoulders go up, where you genuinely believe that he's in Hell. He's not pleased with himself. He's not congratulating himself on how clever he is. They're not crocodile tears, either. I think the accident that happened contributed in a way that nobody could have ever forseen. Certainly, you would never do that in order to make a performance work. But it certainly made Richard very real.

Given the fact that the film is ostensibly about Andy Garcia's character, how did he react to all the attention Richard Gere received when the film was released?
I think it must have been very frustrating for him. He behaved very well. He's a gentleman, and he was very supportive of the film. I think he could also see that the film was a more interesting film for its duality, than had it been the more mono macho Latino cop film which was the one-line concept that Paramount had before it was made. I think he's a remarkable actor. You get really spoiled when you deal with two actors like Andy Garcia and Richard Gere. As well as Laurie Metcalf, Nancy Travis, Annabella Shiora, and William Baldwin. You come to accept that standard of acting as being the way it should be. You don't quite realize that they're all exceptionally good actors in different ways. That's what made it interesting.

I noticed that there are very few close-ups in the film. Why is that?
I used a lot of long lenses because I thought that was the best way to photograph Los Angeles. The story was so much about: Was Richard everywhere? It was almost like a police surveillance camera. I happen to like that long-lens feel. In hot, bright environments, I think it's very strong. It gives you a sense of tension.

How did the actors regard this?
Both Richard and Andy religiously went to dailies, and so very quickly got a sense of what I was doing stylistically. They were very much in tune with that. The first scene we shot was the

fight outside City Hall, which is on a 600 and 1000mm lens. The lens is so long that it needs a special support. We were using those lenses, and on a dolly, so we were getting this movement as well. It was a very strange effect. For them to film it – they couldn't see anyone on the crew; we were miles away. And they had mikes, so you got this very casual, very relaxed quality which was fantastic. I made them look through the camera, so they knew that they were relatively close up; they were mid-body shots. I think it's important with actors that you let them know how you're photographing them. On *Liebstraum* it was very difficult with Kevin Anderson to make him understand sometimes that it was a close-up because the camera seemed so far away.

Liebestraum is your own script, and yet it's also a thriller and it's also set outside England. I would have thought it would have been more personal.
My most comfortable performances as an actor in *The People Show* were always ones in which I was slightly removed from the action and was watching it. The characters I tend to write tend to be outsiders who come into a situation and react, rather than come in and create things that other people react to. So, I tend to write things where people return to some kind of structure that represented a home, or some kind of

approximation of a house or womb-like environment, and they find that things are different. I'm interested in how they react to that whole thing. Like the soldier in *The House*. In *Stormy Monday*, the Sean Bean character is coming through town, he's not really a part of it, but he happens upon a series of events that then draw him in. And then he carries on. Basically, it's a sense of always passing through something. A journey. And never quite resolving that journey. In all of the endings I've written, the characters are unresolved. In *Stormy Monday* Melanie and Sean Bean have shared something, they're still together at the end of the film, but you don't get the feeling that they'll stay together. The characters will then move on.

But at the end of Liebestraum *you do get the feeling that something has been resolved because they have consummated the relationship.*
I think *Liebestraum* is important for me, in that it's a growing-up script in the sense that only by the two of them getting together do they give themselves the potential to carry on and go somewhere else – not keep returning to the house, not keep returning to that mother/father situation.

The fact that Paul doesn't shoot them allows them to go beyond the situation. The gesture he makes is quite important, isn't it?
Yes. I think his gesture is as important as theirs. His story is as interesting as theirs, even though he is a secondary character. I found him immensely sympathetic – the kind of husband who can't quite make it work.

Isn't that partly a tribute to Bill Pullman's performance?
Absolutely. Bill Pullman gave levels to that performance and that character which were beyond my expectations. With a lesser actor I would have accepted a lesser interpretation because he would have fulfilled the crude requirements of the part, which is to be a pivot, to be something you were frightened of and who you thought would come back and repeat the violence of the past. To get more dimensions from an actor, and to get a sympathetic reading to that extent, gives you so much more ambiguity. It's better for me, but for a general audience, I'm told, it makes things more complicated, and maybe not as satisfying because they don't know where their sympathies should lie. But for me, you're getting more for your money.

Certainly, as far as Kim Novak is concerned, you are definitely getting more than you ever would have expected.

Kim Novak is one of those actors who means it. If she goes for something, she means it. As a director you have to work very closely with her. With Kim Novak, the problem was holding her down to a believable state of terminal cancer. She's one of the healthiest women I've met in my life, with colossal reserves of strength. She has this energy and enthusiasm to do something, but, at the same time, not a great technique.

You mean that in the course of making all those films, she didn't develop a technique?
She wasn't allowed to. One of her problems is that she is aware that she was used as a sexual iceberg image. It was a complete surprise to me when I discovered this incredibly sensual extrovert. Not at all the cool, frigid blonde. Nothing could be further from the truth. But, basically, she was put into sexy clothes and told to stare blankly into the camera. So, she has this tremendous frustration that she wants to be an actress; she wants to be a great actress. Given an opportunity like *Liebestraum*, where she's got a role where she's dying and she wants to express herself, then this urge to act and to do this death justice is overwhelming.

The energy that came out of her was not at all compatible with my view of this terminally ill woman who, I felt, barely had the strength to speak and then had to gasp for breath. Getting her in each scene to the level of exhaustion and pathos – because pathos is not a natural characteristic of Kim Novak; she's a fighter – required a great amount of patience. Just sticking with a scene until it was right. After you've been in a small hospital room, with her in bed, for three hours doing one scene, and she's done it quite well – your instincts are to say: Look, let's get out here, let's move on to the next scene. But there's another part of you saying: No, it could be better than this. So, you say: We'll go again. And then everyone starts to look at their watch and you start to feel all those pressures that you're somehow holding everyone up. That's the funny thing about making a film. That's why you're there. But, at the same time, you sometimes have the feeling that the reason you're there is to move on to the next scene.

Was there any problem about getting her to use the coarse language required by the script?
No. There was a very funny moment – there's only a remnant of it in the film – where she finds out from reading the newspaper that she's in the town where the murders originally

happened; she'd been so doped up she hadn't been aware that the hospital was in the same town. So, she has a fit and tries to get out of bed. And then her son walks into the room, and at that moment, especially because of the physical resemblance, she focuses on him as if he were her husband and starts to scream at him. In the original script it said a stream of filthy language comes out of her. She said to me: I'm having difficulty getting into this. I don't really know quite how to do it. And she tried it and it wasn't really working. And then I had this idea. I said: Is there anybody in your past, perhaps in your film career, who you feel totally exploited you, and who you've never forgiven? And suddenly her eyes opened and she said: All right. Don't say anything else. So, we did the scene and this incredible stream of violent, repressed anger came out of her. It was almost too hard to watch.

Liebestraum *is suffused with sex and death.*
The link between sex and death is a very strong and fascinating one to explore. When people close to us die, the sexual urge becomes very strong as an affirmation of being alive. In *Liebestraum*, the character Nick finds himself in a situation where he is visiting his mother, a mother he's never met before, a mother who is obsessed with sexual guilt and jealousy for her husband/son. So, he finds himself in a situation where he's presented with the chance to be promiscuous: he doesn't really know why, but it's a fascinating world to be drawn into. So, what I tried to do in the film is not to play it in a particularly sexual way, but to try and charge the atmosphere.

There is also the fatalistic aspect of sex. People are fated to get together and it's not necessarily to do with a kind of 1960s idea of sex being good, clean fun. The cleaner and more wholesome you make sex, the less interesting it becomes. It also demeans it as the strongest and most basic instinct we have, and separates it into a containable compartment – which American film has done.

Obviously, that was brought home to you when you had the preview in the US and the film was deemed too offensive
The script in this volume is the script of the film that I took to a preview in New York. I was convinced that it was the finished film. It was the closest I could get in editing, post-production, dubbing, music, and so on, to the vision I had of the film, based on the material I had collected throughout shooting. Obviously, I had got very used to the imagery, having written it, shot it,

and edited it. To me it was just normal. I knew some of it was shocking for a first-time viewer, but not that shocking. I thought there was a seamless quality to the way the film was put together, that it flowed, and that the flow of the film would get you across what were the bumps – the shocking scenes.

The scene in the whore-house, as scripted – although it functions, in a sense, like a one-act play and can be lifted, as it has been, completely out of the film – had an enormously important role to play psychologically, for the leading character, Nick. His experience with these prostitutes – which had to do with the smell of women, the taste of women, and the establishing of his character in terms of how he behaved in the situation – was not at all like something out of *Tom Jones*. In other words, it was not a rollicking yarn where a 'real man' would go in and roger those prostitutes and come out and say: I managed to fuck ten of them, how did you do? Nick was very submissive and intimidated by these strong women, who also confronted him with the flip-side of the coin of how men would like women to behave, which is as demure rape victims. No, these were women who came forward and said: What would you like? They were very aggressive. And I thought it set a tone in the film which was sort of outrageous, from which the character then had to live through the rest of the film, and go through a sort of romance, and deal with his mother, and ultimately come to terms with an image which had already occurred in that scene. But at the preview the audience were horrified by the scene. They were so offended and uncomfortable, and made so hostile by having to watch this scene, that it was impossible to watch the rest of the film. It turned into a complete circus, with people shouting and leaving. There was this incredible aggression coming from the audience.

So, what did you do?
Well, first I recut the film, keeping the scene in. I tried to make the scene stronger. I tried to make it more obvious why the scene was there. But, on viewing that myself, I felt very dissatisfied. Suddenly, the scene did seem incredibly crude, which I had never seen it as being before. So, there were two choices. Either go back to the previewed film and keep it exactly as it was – at least I was happy with it. Or to radically recut the film, and take out the whore-house in its entirety. Which is what I did.

Maybe because you're still involved with it, but Liebestraum *seems to be your most personal film.*
I think it is. There are things in *Liebestraum* that when I came to write certain scenes I thought: Oh no, I can't really put that in. It's a little bit too – not only personal – but a little bit too intimate. It was quite a barrier to cross to actually write the film. But then, having written the film, it's fine. There's no problem about it any more. The interesting thing about film-making is that you do work these things out. And only by making these things as films, do you move on from them and, in a sense, become richer. You look at other people's work, like Bergman. He's worked through all kinds of strange emotional statements that he's put on film and then gone on to something else.

And so what are you going on to?
I think I'll be able to make films with children in them soon. I've never made a film with children, apart from *The House*, but that was a ghost. Dealing with the relationship between couples and their children would be very interesting, and I've always been very frightened of that because it's such a strong emotion. But in *Liebestraum*, I think I've managed to work through an adult/childhood problem, which is just getting past your own parents. I'm convinced that the age you are at any given time is not the age you can deal with in a film. You need to be ten years older, you need that perspective.

What is interesting is that although the three feature films are all very different, they also seem to inhabit the same world.
I get attracted to material that is very different to what I've done before, but then, very quickly, find the darkness in it and start to work on that as the key thing in the plot. So nothing would ever remain light completely. I think that any film I make will have an element of darkness in it.

Liebestraum was first shown in the US in the autumn of 1991.

The cast included:

NICK KAMINSKY	Kevin Anderson
JANE KESSLER	Pamela Gidley
PAUL KESSLER	Bill Pullman
MRS ANDERSON	Kim Novak
SHERIFF RICKER	Graham Beckel
BARNETT RALSTON IV	Zach Grenier
DR PARKER	Thomas Kopache
MARY PARKER	Catherine Hicks
NURSE/WHORE	Anne Lange
MIKE	Jack Wallace

Costume Designer	Sharon Simonaire
Editor	Martin Hunter
Production Designer	Waldemar Kalinowski
Post Production Supervisor	Virginia Allan
Music	Mike Figgis
Director of Photography	Juan Ruiz Anchia
Co-Producer	Michael Flynn
Producer	Eric Fellner
Writer and Director	Mike Figgis

An Initial production for Pathe Pictures

LIEBESTRAUM

As the credits appear on black we hear the sound of a violent thunderstorm. The perspective is from inside a building. We hear voices.

VOICE 1: Goodnight. Have a good weekend, Mr Munsen.
VOICE 2: Thanks. You too. I'll lock up.
    (*Fade up on:*)

INT. MUSIC STORE. NIGHT

We see a couple of grand pianos in half light. The shadow of a man comes into shot and he turns off lights. The camera starts to move and we see more of the music store. The man comes into shot and turns out the remaining lights by the counter. He walks to the doorway of an office and hesitates for a moment in the light coming from within before going inside.

Titles on black. The thunder and rain intensifies.

INT. OFFICE. NIGHT

The man's hands come into tight shot. He has a 78 record which he places on to a portable, stainless-steel phonograph. His hands shake as he places the needle on to the record. The music begins. It is Liebestraum by Earl Bostic. This is an early 1950s' jazz version based on Liszt's melody.

The camera tilts up and just before we cut to a new angle we catch a glimpse of a woman in white on the other side of the room.

ANGLE

We see the man in shadow looking to camera. The woman in white walks into shot and spins. Tight shot on her feet in high heels as she hesitates and then begins walking deliberately towards the man. Tight shot on her hands as she begins unbuttoning her blouse. Tight shot of their feet as his two-tone shoes go between her high heels. Titles on black. The perspective of the storm changes to exterior.

3

EXT. STREET. NIGHT

An impressive four-storey cast-iron building fills the frame. The rain is very heavy. In the foreground a black period Cadillac comes to a halt.

TIGHT REVERSE ANGLE *shows the driver to be in his mid-thirties with a moustache and a hat. He looks up at the building.*

INT. OFFICE

The man and woman are making love against a desk. They tear at each other's clothes and he caresses her breasts.

EXT. STREET

The Cadillac drives out of shot and the camera slowly zooms in on the one lit window.

INT. OFFICE

The couple making love on the desk. As the camera pulls back we see that they are being reflected in a photograph of the cast-iron building.

EXT. REAR OF THE BUILDING

A large truck with the name Ralston is parked. The Cadillac comes around the corner and stops. The headlights are switched off.

INT. OFFICE

The camera slowly zooms in on the phonograph, the record spinning.

The lovers reflected in the phonograph.

Zoom in tighter on the phonograph.

EXT. REAR OF BUILDING

The MAN IN THE HAT *walks towards the building through the rain. He opens a door and goes inside.*

INT. BUILDING. FIRE STAIRS

The MAN IN THE HAT *climbs the stairs wearily and pauses by a large window. Outside a freight train is passing. He looks up and then exits frame. In the distance we can hear the sound of the record finishing. The camera zooms in on the train.*

In black we hear the sound of lovemaking mixed with the sound of the phonograph-needle trapped in the play out groove of the record. A door opens slowly and we see into the office. On the far side are the lovers.

MAN: This is crazy.

WOMAN: Don't stop. Stay in me . . . come in me . . . tell me
    you love me . . . say it.

CLOSE UP *on the record spinning.*

MAN: I love you.

WOMAN: Then make a baby in me. (*Close up of the* WOMAN's
    *face. She screams. We hear a loud gunshot. Medium shot of the
    two of them as he takes a bullet hit in his back. A 78 record
    hits the tiled floor and shatters . . . Very tight shot of the record
    spinning. We hear the* WOMAN *screaming . . . a second
    gunshot. Tight shot of her face as she is hit . . . One of her
    shoes drops to the tiled floor . . . Tight shot of the record
    spinning . . . Her hand pushes a pile of records off the desk
    and she falls across frame . . . The records fall and smash . . .
    The spinning record slows up and stops. We can read the label.
    Liebestraum by Earl Bostic and his orchestra on the King
    record label. We hear a third gunshot.
    Fade to black. Silence for a moment and then the sound of a
    train in a tunnel.*)

5

TITLE: THIRTY YEARS LATER

INT. CARRIAGE. DAY

The train comes out of the tunnel and we see a man just waking from a sleep. This is NICK KAMINSKY. *He is in his early thirties, conservatively dressed in a suit. His tie is loosened. He is a good-looking man, but not in a conventional way. All around him are newspapers and pages of handwritten notes. The paper is the Sunday* New York Times. *There is an announcement from the Amtrack* GUARD.

GUARD (*Voice-over*): Ladies and gentlemen, we will shortly be arriving in Elderstown. Next stop will be Elderstown. Passengers for Dearville, Rostock and Bellingham are requested . . .

    (KAMINSKY *begins tidying his papers.*)

EXT. HOSPITAL. AFTERNOON

A yellow cab pulls up in front of a large Gothic building. A sign tells us that this is the Ralston Memorial Hospital. NICK *pays the cab driver and picks up his bags.*

6

INT. HOSPITAL

NICK *steps out of a lift and two nurses in nuns' habits smile at him. The camera tracks with him as he walks to a reception desk. A* NURSE *looks up from her work.*
NURSE: Can I help you?
NICK: I've come to see Mrs Anderson.
NURSE: Visiting time is not for another hour. Are you a relative?
NICK: I'm her son.

INT. WARD. AFTERNOON

NICK *and the* NURSE *come into the ward which has ten beds. The camera tracks with* NICK *as he walks from bed to bed, stopping to look at the faces of the women, all of whom are sleeping. After the fourth he turns to the* NURSE.
NICK: Which one . . . which one is my mother? (*The* NURSE *points at a bed.*)
NURSE: That one . . . I'll be outside. Please don't disturb any of the patients.

CUT TO: ANGLE

NICK *walks into shot and looks down at his* MOTHER. *He looks away and then back.*

ANGLE. HIS POINT OF VIEW

Her skin is very delicate, her hair is fine and prematurely grey. She is in her early fifties. She is clearly very ill, but still beautiful.

INT. DOCTOR'S OFFICE. AFTERNOON

DR PARKER *is seated behind a large desk. A lean man wearing steel rimmed glasses.*
DR PARKER: Your mother is a very sick woman, Mr Anderson.
NICK: Kaminsky . . . my name is Kaminsky. My mother and I have different names.
(DR PARKER *looks at the file in front of him.*)
DR PARKER: Ah . . . yes . . . of course.
NICK: I'd like a private room for her.
(PARKER *is a little uncomfortable.*)
DR PARKER: Mr Kaminsky . . . your mother has only the basic insurance. In fact . . . she's over her credit limit . . .

NICK: Just give her a private room, OK? I'll take care of
   everything.
DR PARKER: All right.
NICK: Does my mother know anyone in Elderstown? Does she
   have any friends here?
DR PARKER: Not that I know of.
NICK: Then why was she moved here?
DR PARKER: She was in a very small hospital . . . about two
   hundred miles from here. Here, at Ralston Memorial we
   can offer the very latest in medical care . . .
NICK: How long?
DR PARKER: We are doing everything we can.
NICK: How long?
   (PARKER *looks very tired suddenly.*)
DR PARKER: I'd say a week . . . more or less.

INT. HOTEL ROOM. EVENING

*On the wall is an old black and white photograph which has been
torn in half. A young woman is smiling at the camera. A man's arm
around her shoulder.*

ANGLE

NICK *walks in from the shower naked, towelling his hair. He looks
pretty good, his body's in good shape. He walks to the window and
looks out at the view. The camera moves in behind him and we see
the cast-iron building featured in the opening sequence. Now the
building is semi-derelict, the windows boarded up. On the roof of the
building are huge metal letters spelling out R.A.L.S.T.O.N.*

EXT. MAIN STREET. NIGHT

The street is deserted as NICK *walks out of Schmidt's Diner. He
stops for a moment and looks at something off-camera.*

ANGLE

The Ralston Building at night. NICK *walks into the shot and
approaches the boarded up entrance of the building. He taps the
façade which gives off a hollow, metallic sound.*
NICK: Cast-iron!

INT. LOBBY. RALSTON BUILDING. NIGHT

We see NICK *peering into the dark interior of the lobby. The camera pans into the darkness and we just make out the face of a mannequin.*

INT. LOBBY OF THE HOTEL. NIGHT

The camera moves in with NICK *as he approaches the desk. The* DESK CLERK *is attending to a man and woman.* NICK *waits and his attention is caught by the couple's two children. They in turn stare at* NICK. *The girl is about fourteen. Her skin is very white, her hair red and long. The boy is younger but also very pale. The* DESK CLERK *gives* NICK *his key.*

DREAM: *A dead tree against a night sky. White mist moves slowly. The camera tilts down and we see the girl and the boy from the lobby. The boy faces the camera but the girl is looking away. A tyre on a rope is attached to one of the branches and it swings slowly. A white picket fence defines this long and narrow garden which stops just short of a railway track. A freight train passes from left to right and the girl turns to face camera. She has her hands behind her back. As she begins to walk towards camera we begin to track back. We hear* NICK's *voice very closely mic'd. (We do not hear the train.)*
NICK (*Voice-over*): Give it back to me.
GIRL: Give it back to me.
BOY: Give it back to me.
NICK: Give it back to me . . . please. (*She continues to mimic him as she walks towards camera. The train continues to pass but we don't hear the sound of the train in any realistic way. The train is back lit and shafts of light come through the gaps in the freight containers illuminating the girl's face as she gets closer.* NICK's *voice now has an edge of panic in it.*)
NICK: Give it to me or I'll tell my mom and dad.

IMAGE: *A close-up of the torn photograph that we saw earlier. It holds for a very short time. When we return to the garden image we see an older man and woman in shadow, close to the camera.*
GIRL: They're not your mom and dad . . .

IMAGE: *We see* NICK'S MOTHER *as she is now but in the same pose as in the photograph, a man's arm around her shoulder.*

9

GIRL'S VOICE (*cont'd*): . . . your mother's a crazy woman, everyone knows that. (*On the soundtrack the phrase 'crazy woman' repeats over and over and is mixed with a banging noise and laboured breathing that becomes sexual . . .*)

INT. HOTEL ROOM. NIGHT

NICK *fights his way out of the dream, and as he opens his eyes we realize that it is the sound of a couple making love in the next room, the bed head is banging against the partition wall. The woman is making a lot of noise, the man is silent apart from the odd low grunt. The passion increases and* NICK *gets out of bed and switches on the* TV, *turning up the volume to drown the noise. He flicks through the stations until he finds an old black and white film –* Invasion of the Bodysnatchers. NICK *watches as the hero discovers that his girl has fallen asleep and become one of the bodysnatchers.*
WOMAN: I went to sleep, Miles, and it happened.
MAN: Oh, Becky.
WOMAN: They were right.
MAN: I should never have left you.
WOMAN: Stop acting like a fool, Miles, and accept us. (NICK *looks out of the window at the building and the camera begins a slow zoom towards the second floor window where the murders took place. On* TV *the voices continue . . .*)
MAN: No . . . never . . .
WOMAN (*shouting*): He's in here . . . he's in here . . . get him. (*The camera ends its zoom tight on the window and we fade to black.*)

TITLE: MONDAY

EXT. STREET. DAY

Workmen are busy on the Ralston Building. We see tools being hauled up in a bucket on a pulley and a man in a hard hat leaning out to haul them in on the roof. As he does so he supports himself on the metal letters. We get a sense of danger from a combination of the height and the almost casual way that the workman behaves.

ANGLE. WIDE SHOT OF THE BUILDING

The empty bucket is coming down for more tools. A man steps into the foreground of the shot and looks around. He is in his early to mid thirties. He is wearing a suit. There is a tough but likeable quality about him. This is PAUL KESSLER.

PAUL: Where's Buddy . . . Hey . . . Buddy.

ANGLE

NICK *looking at the activity. Something takes his eye and he walks until he is standing next to* PAUL *who is talking to his foreman* BUDDY. BUDDY *walks away and* NICK *continues to stare at* PAUL. *He smiles as* PAUL *looks at him.*

NICK: Hello, Paul!

PAUL: Kaminsky . . . Kaminsky . . . Nick fucking Kaminsky!

NICK: How are you, man?

PAUL: What the fuck are you doing here?

NICK: Just what I was going to ask you. I thought you were in Chicago.

PAUL: I was, I was . . . but then I came down here . . . got an offer I couldn't refuse . . . so here I am. In Elderstown. But what about you? Jesus Christ . . . the last thing . . . you were teaching some architectural . . . post-doctoral . . . pre-sexual type thing in upstate New York . . . right?

NICK: I am. (PAUL *suddenly becomes very cautious.*)

PAUL: You're not here to check this out, are you? (NICK *looks suitably puzzled.*)

NICK: Check what out? I'm here to see my mother, she's in hospital. (PAUL *looks highly relieved.*)

PAUL: That's too bad . . . (*A large truck causes them to move off the street and on to the sidewalk.*)

ANGLE

Another bucket of tools is seen going up on the pulley. The workman leaning out to guide the ropes.

ANGLE. NICK AND PAUL

PAUL: Hey . . . I read your books . . . well, I didn't exactly read 'em. But I bought 'em . . . my wife read 'em. Says she enjoyed 'em (*laughs*) but you never can believe a woman . . .

ANGLE. THEIR POINT OF VIEW OF THE BUILDING

PAUL (*Voice-over*): So what do you think of this?

NICK: Jesus, it's beautiful, isn't it. How long is it going to take?

PAUL: Four days . . . a week at the most. This is a great crew.

NICK: A week? To do what?

PAUL: Demolish it!

ANGLE

Camera, long lens, follows a black stretch limo as it approaches the building.

NICK (*Voice-over*): Oh come on . . . You're joking.

PAUL: This fucker's coming down. (PAUL *excuses himself and goes off to talk to* BUDDY *while* NICK *looks dazed and stares up at the building. The limo comes to a halt and the tinted window opens to reveal a strange-looking man with a mournful face. He is in his middle thirties. He stares intently at the activity. This is* BARNETT RALSTON.)

ANGLE. TOP OF THE BUILDING

We see the workman's boots as he leans over . . .

ANGLE

BARNETT RALSTON *looks up at the top of the building.*

ANGLE

PAUL *and* BUDDY *suddenly notice* RALSTON.

PAUL: What the fuck is he doing here?

ANGLE

The WORKMAN's *point of view as he leans out from the building.*

ANGLE

Extreme close up of a section of rusted metal frame. A bolt sheers off under the pressure of the workman leaning on it.

ANGLE

NICK *watching* PAUL *and* BUDDY.

ANGLE

BARNETT RALSTON *looking up at . . .*

LOW ANGLE *of the building . . . The letter 'N' is falling from the top of the building.*

ANGLE

NICK *looks up and sees the letter. He runs towards* PAUL *and* BUDDY.

NICK: Watch it . . . (*He pushes them to the ground as the letter crashes through the scaffolding and smashes into the sidewalk in a cloud of dust.*)

ANGLE

BARNETT RALSTON *caresses his face with a piece of white cloth the way a small child comforts himself with a blanket-edge.* NICK *helps* PAUL *to his feet. The* WORKMAN *is pulled to safety by his mate on the roof. The black limo cruises away.* PAUL *hugs* NICK.

PAUL: I owe you one.

NICK: It's lucky that I looked up.

PAUL: No . . . I owe you one.

NICK: Well . . . don't worry about it.

PAUL: What are you doing tonight?

NICK: Nothing . . . but you don't have to . . .

PAUL: I'm having a party . . . it's my wife's birthday . . . you gotta come.

CUT TO: INT. HOSPITAL. PRIVATE ROOM. DAY

A door opens and a NURSE *comes in carrying red roses.*

NURSE: These are beautiful, Mr Kaminsky. (*She puts them on a bedside table and we see* NICK *sitting in a chair, a book on his knee.*) That's the call button, just press it if you need anything. (*She leaves.* NICK *stares at his* MOTHER, *who is asleep in the half-light from the window.* NICK *looks down at his book.*

ANGLE

We see that it is a textbook on cast-iron architecture. The page he is looking at has a photograph of the Ralston Building. NICK *settles in his chair and closes his eyes.*

CUT TO: EXT. HOSPITAL. AFTERNOON

The black limo pulls up outside the hospital. A chauffeur gets out and opens the passenger door.

INT. MOTHER'S ROOM. AFTERNOON

NICK *has been sleeping. His eyes open and it takes him a moment or two to remember where he is. He glances over to where his* MOTHER *is and his face registers surprise.*

HIS POINT OF VIEW: *She is awake and is staring at him, has been for some time. It is a long time before she speaks.*

MOTHER: You're Nick?

13

NICK: Yes. (*She begins to turn away from him, her face twisted with emotion. She starts to cry and covers her face with her hands, her whole body shaking.* NICK *is alarmed and doesn't know what to do. He shouts for the* NURSE.

CUT TO: INT. TAXI. NIGHT

NICK *is sitting in the back of the taxi in the dark. The only light is from passing cars and street lights. We only ever see the driver in the rear mirror. The scene has a strange quality.* NICK *is holding a bunch of red roses. He holds them close to his face to smell them.*
TAXI DRIVER: You OK?
NICK: I'm fine . . . going to a party.
TAXI DRIVER: Look like you already went. (*Pause.*) Mind if I ask you a personal question? Are you in show biz? I mean . . . I feel like I know you . . . You in TV or what? (NICK *looks at him.*)
NICK: What?

CUT TO: EXT. ELDERSTOWN SUBURB. NIGHT

The taxi drives off leaving NICK *alone in the dark.* PAUL'S *house is large and there are no other houses near it. It's many miles out of town.* NICK *stands still and listens to the sounds of a swinging party that come from the brightly lit windows.*

CUT TO: INT. PAUL'S HOUSE. NIGHT

NICK *walks into a room full of party people. He is carrying the roses. He looks around the room but there is no sign of* PAUL. *We see* NICK *drinking, watching the guests who are mainly his age. Two men stare at him and* NICK *finishes his drink and goes off in search of* PAUL. *He is looking a little the worse for wear.*

INT. CORRIDOR. NIGHT

As NICK *comes to the end of the corridor he sees a* WAITER *coming out of the kitchen.*
WAITER: Si . . . si Mrs Kessler.
(*The* WAITER *walks past* NICK *with a tray of food and* NICK *walks to the kitchen door and looks in. A woman is checking something in the oven. She is wearing a simple black dress cut low over her breasts. She has very short hair, like a boy. She is*

14

very beautiful. She is unaware that NICK *is watching her. He
finds her extremely attractive from this first moment. She moves
out of his sight.*)

NICK: Hello. (*She looks around the corner and sees* NICK. *The
following exchange has a very intense quality.* NICK *is quite
aggressive.*)

WOMAN: Hello.

NICK: You're Paul's wife?

WOMAN: Yes . . . I am.

NICK: What's your name?

WOMAN: Jane.

NICK: Happy birthday, Jane.

JANE: Thanks . . . (JANE *moves out a little further to get a better
look at* NICK.) I recognize you . . . from that photograph in
your book . . . yeah, you're Nick.

NICK: Yeah . . . Where's Paul?

JANE: He's around.

NICK: These are for you. (*He hands her the roses.*)

JANE: That's very kind of you. (JANE *takes the roses and smells
them, stares at* NICK.)

NICK: They're looking a bit sad. I hope it's not too late.

JANE: I don't think so. I can fix sad roses. (*She hears a door
opening and looks away as . . .*)

ANGLE

PAUL *comes into the room.*

PAUL: Honey . . . you about ready because . . . (*He becomes*

15

aware of NICK. JANE *gives* NICK *a deep look before turning away.*)

PAUL: Nick Kaminsky has arrived. Great . . . great. You won't regret it . . . it's going to be a great party. You met my wife? (JANE *turns from the sink where she is putting the roses in a vase.*)

JANE: Yes.

CUT TO: INT. STAIRS

NICK *and* PAUL *climb the stairs.* PAUL *is telling how cheap house prices are in Elderstown. They pass a drunk who is giving a girl the eye. This is* SHERIFF RICKER.

INT. MAIN ROOM PARTY

NICK *and* PAUL *watch the action from the entrance to the loft, which is being used as the main party room.*

NICK: Can I ask you a favour?

PAUL: Sure, anything, you saved my life.

NICK: That building you're going to pull down.

PAUL: The Ralston Building?

NICK: I'd like to have a closer look, maybe write something while I'm in town. Is that possible?

PAUL: You aren't gonna say something snotty about me destroying the cultural heritage of Elderstown or anything like that, are you?

NICK (*laughing*): No . . . no . . . Paul, it's just that it's a beautiful building . . . I'd like to write something.

PAUL: You aren't gonna inflict any guilt for this?

NICK: I promise.

PAUL: OK, we're going in there at eight o'clock. You're welcome to join us.

NICK: Why was it closed in the first place? (*A hand falls on* NICK's *shoulder. He turns and sees* DR PARKER *from the hospital.*)

DR PARKER: Young man . . . we meet again! I didn't realize you knew our distinguished host.

NICK: Paul and I went to college together . . .

PAUL: . . . ten years ago . . . and this fucker shows up on Main Street!

DR PARKER: Quite a coincidence . . . may I introduce my wife . . ?

(*A sexy blonde turns around. She seems a little stoned and is swaying to the music. She is a lot younger than her husband. She looks bored with the party.*)

DR PARKER: Mary . . . Mr . . . unh?

NICK: Kaminsky.

DR PARKER: Mr Kaminsky's mother is in our care at the hospital.

MARY: Good luck!

(*There is an awkward silence while* PAUL *tries to make it a joke.*)

NICK: Are you in the same profession as your husband, Mrs Parker?

MARY: It's kind of connected. I work at the hospital. (*She begins to laugh and* NICK *laughs with her.*)

NICK: Are you a doctor? (DR PARKER *comes in on their conversation.*)

DR PARKER: Mary works in the pathology department, down in the morgue. Fascinating world.

MARY: It has its moments. (*She slides up to* PAUL.) Paul . . . are you going to dance with me? (*It is clear that there is some private drama being played out here.*)

ANGLE

JANE *coming up the stairs. She looks over at them* . . .

PAUL (*Voice-over*): I've got some hosting to catch up on . . . but Nick here used to be quite the mover.

ANGLE

MARY PARKER *stares right back at* JANE. NICK *tries to get out of dancing.*

DR PARKER: You'd be doing me a big favour. (MARY PARKER *walks off without even bothering to check if* NICK *is following. He finishes his drink and joins her near to where* JANE *is talking to* SHERIFF RICKER. NICK *is a little unsteady on his feet. She slowly spins around in a stoned way.*)

NICK: You're a really good dancer. (*She looks at him for the first time.*)

MARY: I'm an even better fuck. (*The camera moves to* JANE. *She and* MARY PARKER *stare at each other.*)

CUT TO: INT. BATHROOM

NICK *splashes cold water on to his face and leers at himself in the mirror. Someone is knocking on the door.*

17

INT. MAIN PARTY ROOM

SHERIFF RICKER *pulls a reluctant* JANE *on to the dance floor.*

LANDING. OUTSIDE BATHROOM

NICK *comes out of the bathroom and is reluctant to go back to the party. He sees a partly open door and goes to take a look.*

MAIN PARTY

On the dance floor PAUL *and* MARY PARKER *are deep in conversation.*

LANDING

NICK *walks into a dark room where something has taken his attention.*

DANCE FLOOR

SHERIFF RICKER *spins* JANE *around a little too enthusiastically and she almost loses her balance. She looks a little angry but continues dancing.*

INT. ROOM

We see that the room NICK *is walking into is a photographic darkroom. Lots of photographs are pinned up on the wall and* NICK *looks at them. The camera goes in tight on one of them. It is a window of the Ralston Building.*

DANCE FLOOR

RICKER *is holding* JANE *tight and she is trying to get away from him as another dancer lurches into him and the drink that he is holding goes over* JANE. PAUL *sees what is happening and leaves* MARY *to help* JANE. *He arrives as* RICKER *is trying to dab a napkin on* JANE's *breast.*
PAUL: I'll take it from here . . . you OK?
JANE: I'm fine, how are you? Are you having fun? (JANE *looks over to where* MARY *is standing.*)
PAUL: Yeah . . . a great time.

JANE: Exactly. (JANE *storms off down the stairs.* PAUL *looks a little whipped.*)

INT. DARKROOM

NICK *is looking at the photographs. He hears something and as the camera moves around we see that the darkroom is connected to the bedroom.* JANE *crosses the doorway, taking off her dress. She walks towards the darkroom in her underwear and high heels.* NICK *tries to hide but there is nowhere.*

JANE: Stupid fucking bastard. (*She gets to the sink and turns on the light. She suddenly becomes aware of* NICK *and turns, clutching the dress to her bosom. She is really angry now.*)

JANE: What the hell're you doing in my room?

NICK: I was looking at the photographs. I didn't mean to frighten you . . . They're really very good. (*They stare at each other. She is a little less angry. He is very confused.*)

NICK: Who took them?

JANE: I did!

NICK: They're excellent. (NICK *looks down but makes no effort to leave.*)

JANE: Are you all right?

NICK: My head . . . spinning. There's a lot of people up there . . . had to escape. Excuse me. (JANE *looks at him a little more sympathetically. He heads for the door but takes one last look at the photographs.*)

NICK: Ralston Building . . . right?

JANE: Yes.

NICK: It's beautiful.

JANE: Yes, it is. (NICK *looks at her and smiles.*)

NICK: Cast-iron.

JANE: Mmm.

NICK: I'd better get back down. (*He reaches the door and then comes back.*) I'm really very . . . very sorry. (JANE *smiles at last.*)

JANE: It's OK.

NICK: Goodnight.

JANE: Goodnight.

The PARKERS *are leaving.*

DR PARKER: Say goodnight to Jane for me. I couldn't find her anywhere.

PAUL: Yeah . . . I don't know where she went. Thanks for coming, thanks for the present. Mary . . . goodnight. (NICK *steps in to say goodbye to* PAUL.)

NICK: Quite a party.

PAUL: Yeah. Been a while unh?

NICK: Yeah . . . I'd better get some sleep. Can I phone for a cab?

PAUL: No . . . absolutely not necessary. Pete? (SHERIFF RICKER *is just passing.*) Can you give Nick a ride back into town?

RICKER: Yeah . . . yeah, yeah, yeah. Ready to go? (RICKER *hops from foot to foot.*)

NICK: Well . . . thanks again.

PAUL: Thank you . . . for saving my life.

NICK: Oh fuck you.

PAUL: No . . . see you tomorrow, eight o'clock, sleep well.

CUT TO: EXT. THE HOUSE. NIGHT

RICKER *unzips his fly as he and* NICK *walk to his squad car. He stands next to the driver's door and begins to piss. A couple walk past on the way to their car.*

RICKER: Nice party unh? (*They do not answer*) Republicans! (NICK *waits by the passenger door while* RICKER *carries on pissing. He looks at* NICK.) Get in. It's unlocked. (NICK *does so.* RICKER *carries on.*) I love a good piss. (*After some considerable time* RICKER *finishes and gets into the squad car.*) You can't beat that. (*He starts up the car, guns the engine and drives off at great speed, putting the car into a spin as he goes around the first corner.*)

INT. SQUAD CAR. NIGHT

This is an instant nightmare. RICKER *drives very fast, very badly, using both sides of the road.* NICK *fastens his safety belt,* RICKER *gives him a look of contempt.*

RICKER: You an old friend of the Kesslers?

NICK: I was at college with Paul, this is the first time I've met his wife.

RICKER: She's some hot little bitch unh? If I was Kessler I'd
keep her under lock and key.
NICK: They seem like a happy couple to me. (RICKER *looks at*
NICK, *opens his mouth and roars with laughter. The car starts
to veer across the road* . . . NICK *flinches and at the last
possible moment* RICKER *straightens out.*)
RICKER: I like the way you said that. They seem like a happy
couple. That's great.
NICK: I think we should slow down here.
RICKER: You like Pussy? (*The car heads straight for another car.*
NICK *covers his eyes.*) You like it . . . or you don't like it?
(*At the last moment before collision* RICKER *steers the car out
of trouble.*)
NICK: I like it.
RICKER: You LIKE it . . . I LOVE IT!

EXT. ROAD HOUSE. NIGHT

*The squad car, with all of its emergency lights on, drives into the
parking lot and skids to a halt inches from the entrance to the bar.*

CUT TO: INT. ROAD HOUSE. BROTHEL

*A blind girl is playing the 'Moonlight Sonata'. The camera pans up
and we see* CINDY, *the madam of the brothel, sitting on the bar.
The door opens and* RICKER *comes in, his arm around* NICK. *He
staggers up to* CINDY *and kisses her.*
CINDY: Hi there Mr Ricker. The usual? And what would your
friend like?
RICKER: He'll have the same. (RICKER *hugs* NICK *as* CINDY
pours the drinks.) His name is Nick. Where's Maxine?
CINDY: Out on a date . . . Betty's here, though.
RICKER: She'll do just fine.
CINDY: Betty . . . room nine.

ANGLE

We see BETTY *getting up from a table. Behind her there are another
two girls sitting together on a sofa.* BETTY *smiles a little
apprehensively as* RICKER *turns to leer at her.*
RICKER: They're all clean . . . I have 'em checked out once a
month . . . take your pick, Nick. It's on me. (RICKER *slaps*
BETTY *hard on the bottom.*)
BETTY: Don't do that, it makes a bruise on my butt. (RICKER

21

puts his hand to his mouth in mock surprise and then follows
BETTY *out.* CINDY *gets down off the bar and looks at* NICK
for a moment before going to the table where BETTY *was
sitting. She pours herself a drink.*)

CINDY: Come and sit with us, Nicky. (*He struggles to clear his
head. He finishes his drink and walks over to the table and sits
down opposite* CINDY. *The pianist is working towards the
climax of the piece and the music is getting louder. Suddenly*
CINDY *turns on her and screams.*) Annie . . . you are
depressing the fuck out of everyone. (ANNIE *stops playing.*
MICHELE, *one of the girls on the sofa, looks at* CINDY.)

MICHELE: Take it easy, Cindy. (ANNIE *picks up her glass and
smashes it on the floor.* CINDY *slowly turns to face* NICK
again.)

CINDY: Anything you'd like to do, Nicky? Michele . . . stand
up. Let Nick see you. (MICHELE *gets up and walks over to*
CINDY. *She is wearing a black transparent nightgown. She
leans down so that her face is level with* CINDY's.) Michele's
reputation is built around her mouth. It's big . . . it's
perfect. (*The women look at each other.* MICHELE *sticks out
her tongue and* CINDY *dips her finger into her drink and then
strokes the tongue.* MICHELE *stands up and flicks her fingers
open over her breasts. Her nails are very long and bright red.*)
Sit down, Michele. Barbara . . . come here. (BARBARA
stays put on the sofa and stares insolently back at CINDY.)

BARBARA: No. (CINDY *looks very angry as she gets up and walks over to the sofa.*)

CINDY: Get up! (BARBARA *slowly gets up and walks over to the table.*) What are you, Barbara? (BARBARA *leans over and leans on the table.*)

BARBARA: I'm a bad girl, ma'am.

CINDY: She can be so unpleasant . . . but Nicky . . . You don't have to put up with any fucking nonsense from this whore . . . (CINDY *walks over to the table.*) You just put her across your knee . . . (*She slaps her hard on the bottom and* BARBARA *smiles at* NICK. CINDY *sits down and they both stare at* NICK. ANNIE *has started to play again. It is the last slow section of* Liebestraum.) She has fine qualities as well. Do you like to eat?

NICK: Yes.

CINDY: Let him try some, Barbara. (BARBARA *stands, hands her cigarette to* CINDY *and then pulls up her dress and puts her hand between her legs for a moment. She then offers the hand to* NICK.) Try some. (BARBARA *advances on* NICK *and touches his lips with her fingers*) Come on Nicky . . . try some. (NICK *looks up at* BARBARA *and then takes the fingers in his mouth and sucks them. The hand is withdrawn as the music concludes.* NICK *has his eyes closed. He opens them.*)

Fade to black.

INT. RALSTON BUILDING. DAY

A series of shots show the dusty interior of the building in a gloomy half-light. In the distance we can hear the sounds of activity as PAUL's *crew begin to break in.*

TITLE: TUESDAY

EXT. RALSTON BUILDING

A close-up of an oxy-acetaline torch cutting through the metal bars on the main doors of the building. Through the sparks we see JANE *taking photographs of the action.* NICK *walks into shot and watches also.* JANE *becomes aware of him.*

JANE: Good morning.

NICK: Morning. (JANE *takes another photograph.*)

JANE: So what's so special about this building? For you, I mean.

NICK: It's cast-iron. A building like this . . . it's the missing
link in American architecture. (JANE *starts to move away to
get a better angle to photograph*.)
JANE: What do you mean? (NICK *follows her*.)
NICK: Well . . . before the cast-iron building came along . . .
the height of a given structure was governed by the
thickness of the outer, load-bearing walls. The higher the
building . . . the thicker the walls had to be. Eight floors
was about as high as you could go. (JANE *moves again and
he follows her, both looking at the building*.) These buildings
were very popular with the new Barons . . . like Ralston
because you could choose a style . . . Roman . . . Greek
this one's Victorian . . . from a catalogue.
JANE: Unh huh.
NICK: Instant European culture in Elderstown. (NICK *laughs,
warming to the subject as* JANE *takes another picture. He
touches her*.) Come here . . . I'll show you something.

ANGLE

The torch is cutting through the metal.

ANGLE

PAUL *looks at his watch, worried, and then looks up and sees* NICK
and JANE *talking. He looks sad.*

ANGLE

NICK *brings* JANE *to the façade of the building.*
NICK: You see . . . the whole of this front . . . is in sections
. . . it's just bolted together and fixed on to the building.
(JANE *looks at him attentively*.) But all this metal . . . it's
very heavy and it has to be supported. So someone came up
with the bright idea of a metal frame . . . for the entire
building, instead of the traditional bricks and mortar.
JANE: Unh huh.
NICK: With a steel frame . . . all of the stress is shifted away
from the outer walls . . . to the horizontal . . . so that the
support comes from the centre. You can go as high as you
like. (JANE *smiles at him*.)
JANE: Hence the sky-scraper. (NICK *goes a bit quiet and then
looks at her*.)
NICK: You know all this, don't you.

JANE: I read your book on cast-iron. I just wanted to know if
    you were as passionate about it as you seemed.
NICK: I'm passionate about it.
JANE: Good . . . it must be nice to be one of your students.
    (JANE *walks away, leaving* NICK *alone.*)

ANGLE

The torch cuts through the last section of metal and it falls away.

INT. RALSTON BUILDING

*We see a silhouette against the dirty glass of the main doors and then
the doors open, knocking down a mannequin and raising some dust.*
PAUL *and* NICK *and* JANE *come in holding flashlights, followed by*
BUDDY *and the crew. The camera slowly cranes down from a high
position.*
PAUL: Jesus . . . I don't believe this.
JANE: I do.
NICK: This is fantastic . . . did you know all of this stuff was in
    here?
PAUL: No . . . Buddy. Look at this fucking mess. What are we
    going to do?
BUDDY: It's not going to be a problem. I'll bring some dealers
    in.
    (NICK *and* JANE *proceed further into the building.*)
PAUL: Jane, Jane. Where are you going?
JANE: I'm right here.
PAUL: Be careful. I don't know about the floorboards.

ANGLE

A hand wipes away the dust from a store directory.
PAUL (*Voice-over*): OK . . . let's bring some power in here.

EXT. STREET. DAY

A workman starts up a generator.

INT. STORE

*One by one the interior lights come on and we see a whole
department of the store lit up.*

CUT TO: INT. SCHMIDT'S DINER. LUNCHTIME

The place is jumping with the lunchtime crowd. NICK, PAUL *and* JANE *are having a sandwich and a coffee at one of the tables.* NICK *is quite worked up.*

NICK: Paul . . . that's a cast-iron building over there. It's fucking crazy to knock it down. What do these townspeople think?

PAUL: They don't give a shit, they hate the place, it's a bad memory for most of them . . . they'll probably give me a medal.

(JANE *has been listening quietly.*)

JANE: If they don't, the Glendale Development Corporation certainly will. (PAUL *glares at her and there is a flash of something between them. He smashes his fist on to the table and shouts . . .*)

PAUL: The fucking place is coming down. No more crap . . . (PAUL's *bleeper goes off and he reaches for it.*) . . . everything

is done. We have dates, we have contracts. In six months'
time there will be a busy, successful shopping mall, the
Ralston Centre . . . (PAUL *stands and turns his attention to*
NICK.) . . . and one more thing . . . Nick, remember you
promised me last night . . . you are not going to fuck the
whole thing up with this article . . . right? I'm not the bad
guy. (PAUL *goes off to make his call leaving* NICK *and* JANE
together. They are both a little shell-shocked.)
JANE: I'm sorry.

ANGLE. SCHMIDT'S PHONE BOOTH

We see PAUL *on the phone in a booth. He is having a very heated
conversation. We can see from this and the previous scene that he is
under a lot of pressure.*

ANGLE. NICK AND JANE

The outburst has created a kind of intimacy for them. JANE *looks at*
NICK.
JANE: So . . . are you going to write something about the
building?
NICK: I'd like to. I've never seen anything like that before.
JANE: I know.
NICK: How about you? Are you going to photograph that?
     (JANE *smiles.*)
JANE: You bet.

ANGLE. TELEPHONE BOOTH

PAUL *slams the phone down and looks at* NICK *and* JANE *talking
for a moment before setting off.*

ANGLE. TABLE

The waitress is serving coffee as PAUL *arrives. He sits down and
looks a little dejected. He reaches out and touches* JANE.
PAUL: I'm sorry.
JANE: (*Cool*) It's OK . . . what's up?
PAUL: Oh . . . the architect's fucked up again. I've got to go to
Chicago tomorrow.
JANE: For how long?
PAUL: Oh . . . a day . . . maybe two. (NICK *is very
uncomfortable.*)
NICK: I should get to the hospital. (PAUL *turns to him.*)
PAUL: Nick . . . I was thinking. Are you going to need any
photographs for that article? . . . because Jane's work is

very good. (NICK *doesn't quite know how to react. Nor does* JANE.)

CUT TO: INT. HOSPITAL ROOM. AFTERNOON

A screen is removed from around NICK'S MOTHER'*s bed. She looks very drawn and ill. The nurses exit and one of them speaks to* NICK *who is standing by the door watching.*

NURSE: She's been in a lot of pain today. We've just given her some morphine. It'll make her sleepy, I'm afraid. (*The* NURSE *exits.* NICK'S MOTHER *is not yet aware that he is in the room. There is a* TV *at the foot of the bed and she is watching an afternoon 'soap' with the sound down low. She gives off a high nervous energy and her hands tremble and play with the sheets. She looks from the* TV *to the window, the two sources of light in the room.* NICK *waits for a while before speaking.*)

NICK: Hello, Mother. (*She still doesn't look at him.* NICK *goes to the bed and sits next to her. She looks up at him.*)

MOTHER: Jesus . . . (*laughs and shakes her head*) I think you're even prettier than that son of a bitch was. Yes I think so. (NICK *smiles.*) Do you have a cigarette?

NICK: No, I don't.

MOTHER: You don't smoke?

NICK: Sometimes.

MOTHER: He smoked two packs a day. They won't let me smoke here, they say it's bad for my health. Bring me a pack next time you come. (*A pain spasm hits her and her whole body tenses and then relaxes as it passes.*) That's better. Sometimes the pain is like a knife. It's my punishment, you know.

NICK: No . . . stop that . . . you mustn't say that. (*She rests for a while. Her eyes are closed.*)

MOTHER: Nick . . . I asked them to contact you. It must be very upsetting. I'm sorry.

NICK: Don't be. I'm glad you did.

MOTHER: Really?

NICK: Really. How did you find me?

MOTHER: Couple of years ago . . . I was in a bookshop and I saw your picture. I got a real shock. I knew it was you before I saw the name. I have all your books, over there in the drawer. Are you writing another?

NICK: Yes, I am. I'm going to dedicate it to you.

28

MOTHER: I'd be so proud, Nick. (*She takes his hand and there is a very strong feeling between the two of them. She looks up at him, tears in her eyes.*) He was so handsome . . . (*She hesitates for a moment and then decides to carry on.*) One night . . . he came in very late. I was carrying you, I was awake. He came in real quiet so's not to disturb me, so I didn't let on. He slipped into bed . . . was asleep in minutes . . . His hand was there on the pillow between us . . . I gently took it and began to kiss the fingers, one by one. (*She looks at* NICK, *a desperate expression on her face.*) . . . and I could smell the cunt on them. (*She closes her eyes and* NICK *looks away . . . lost.*)

CUT TO: INT. RALSTON BUILDING. LATE AFTERNOON

At first the screen is black and then a camera move reveals a section of the store. JANE *is walking around looking at things to photograph. She sees* NICK, *silhouetted against a window. She hesitates.*

JANE: Nick? (*He turns and* JANE *sees that he is upset.*) Is your mother OK?

NICK: She's . . . (*He can't get anything out. He covers his face with his hands and cries.*)

JANE: Are you all right? (*He shakes his head and turns into the wall. She puts her bag down and goes to him, placing herself between him and the wall. She holds his head as he cries.*) Hey . . . it's all right. (*She kisses him gently. They look at each other for a moment and then he kisses her hard and she responds. They part and he looks away.*)

CUT TO: EXT. SCHMIDT'S DINER. NIGHT

A car drives by.

INT. SCHMIDT'S

PAUL *and* NICK *are sitting at the bar, drinking.* PAUL *seems quite drunk. They clink glasses and drink. A customer eyes* PAUL *cautiously.*

PAUL: Jane used to have really long hair . . . it was beautiful . . . she could sit on it. And then she cut it all off . . . (PAUL *stares into space. He seems quite dangerous.*) She found a pair of black lace panties in the back of my pick-up . . . (*He stares at* NICK *and* NICK *keeps quiet, wondering where all this is leading.* PAUL *signals to the barmaid.*) Diane . . . just one more . . . for the road. And then I have to go home . . . I have to pack . . . did I say that already?

NICK: No. (PAUL's *expression changes, his mood becomes ugly as he turns on* NICK.)

PAUL: I have said that already . . . you fuck. (NICK *takes a drink.* PAUL *slams his glass down on the counter.*) This cast-iron building . . . you can come and go as you please . . . just don't come in Jane. (NICK *starts to protest, looks baffled.* PAUL *puts his arm around* NICK's *shoulders and then pulls him towards him, gently at first and then increasing the pressure around his neck using both hands. He is very strong.*)

NICK: Paul, what are you doing, Paul?

PAUL: I'm fucking serious, Nick. (PAUL *holds him tight for a moment and then lets him go, awkwardly.*) Hey . . . I gotta have one . . . for the road, and then I gotta pack. I . . . already said that once . . . didn't I.

INT. HOTEL ROOM. NIGHT

NICK *falls on to the bed and closes his eyes. The camera moves off the bed into the dark . . .*

IMAGE: JANE *wearing the black dress from the party, spinning around. The camera move takes it to the window and it begins to zoom into the Ralston Building.*

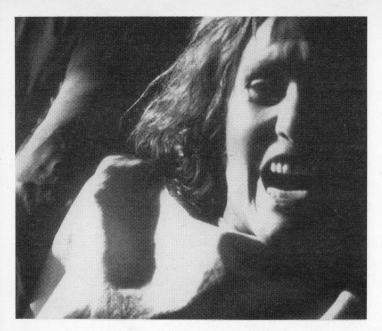

MIX TO: IMAGE: JANE *stops spinning and undoes the strap to her dress. She lowers the top of the dress and cups her breast which is now exposed.*

IMAGE: NICK'S MOTHER, *her face contorted with rage moves her head from side to side.*

IMAGE: JANE *looks directly into the camera whilst caressing her breast.*

MIX TO: IMAGE: *The camera slowly moves over a figure covered in a white sheet. There is some sensual movement under the sheet. The move continues and then reveals* JANE *in bed. Her hand is inside her nightdress, touching her breast and she is just waking from a dream. The camera moves back and we see* PAUL *beside her in bed. His hand is between her legs. She is very aroused. His hand moves up her body and she turns away from him and curls her body up. He rolls on to his back and stares at the ceiling.*

Fade to black.

TITLE: WEDNESDAY

EXT. RALSTON STORE ENTRANCE. MORNING

NICK *opens the main doors and walks into the deserted building.*

INT. RALSTON BUILDING

NICK *walks into one of the rooms and looks around. He sees something and walks towards camera. The camera moves with him and reveals* JANE *who is preparing her cameras. She looks sad. She turns as he approaches.*

NICK: Morning.

JANE: Good morning.

NICK: You're early.

JANE: I . . . wanted to get my equipment set up. I was a little nervous. (*There is a long silence.* NICK *stands behind her, looking at her.*) There's a coffee there for you.

NICK: Thanks. (*As he picks up the coffee she turns to look at him and then turns away again.*)

JANE: You look a little better than Paul did this morning.

NICK: This is a hard drinking town, I don't know how long I'd survive. (NICK *moves right behind* JANE.) What are you nervous about?

JANE: We haven't talked or anything . . . I don't know what you want.

NICK: I don't know either . . . I'd just like to capture everything . . . just the way it is right now.

MONTAGE: *Shots of the building –* JANE *taking photographs –* NICK *watching her work. The music here is a sad piano blues which we will come to associate with* NICK *and* JANE.

ANGLE

JANE *taking a photograph. She is holding a shutter release cable and counting before releasing it.*

JANE: My . . . father . . . was a photographer, weddings, that kind of thing, so I've known how to use a camera since I was very small. I used to help him print . . . I gave it all up when I went to college. (NICK *walks into the shot, looking at what she is photographing.*)

NICK: What made you take it up again? (JANE *looks down at her viewfinder.*)

JANE: Paul.

32

EXT. RALSTON ENTRANCE. DAY

Workmen are carrying out things from the store. Dealers are looking at carpets and furniture and there is a lot of activity as NICK *and* JANE *walk out of the building.* JANE *points at a beaten-up, red pick-up truck.*

JANE: Here.

NICK: A pick-up?

JANE: What did you expect?

NICK: I dunno . . . a Volvo. (*They both get in the pick-up, laughing, and* JANE *starts up the engine and drives off. This is all watched with great interest by* BUDDY, *who is talking to a dealer.*)

EXT. RALSTON MEMORIAL HOSPITAL. DAY

The red pick-up pulls up outside the hospital entrance.

JANE: This must be very difficult for you. Are you very close?

NICK: It's strange . . . I never met my mother before this week. My father was killed in a car accident . . . just before I was born. She went . . . kind of went crazy for a while. (NICK *looks at* JANE) I was adopted. (JANE *looks very startled, turns her head away.*) What?

JANE: I was adopted. (*She changes the subject quickly.*) Is that why you don't drive . . . because of your father? (NICK *starts to get out of the car.*)

NICK: Kind of. I just like being driven around by beautiful women. Thanks for the ride. (*He smiles at her, she at him, closes the door and walks away.*)

CUT TO: INT. HOSPITAL ROOM

From the doorway we see NICK'S MOTHER *in bed. She is very still. We hear footsteps and then* NICK *comes in.*

MOTHER: Hello, Nick. How are you?

NICK: I'm good, how about you?

MOTHER: Just great, much better. Come and sit over here, by me. (NICK *sits by the bed.*) I want to talk to you. I'm not crazy you know . . . (NICK *starts to protest. The camera begins a slow move in on her face.*) I know what's happening inside of me.

NICK: This is a good hospital . . . the best . . .

MOTHER: Don't bullshit me, Nick. It's true isn't it? (NICK's *head drops and he nods. She smiles.*) Did you bring the smokes? (NICK *fishes in his pocket and brings out a bottle of Scotch.*)

NICK: Let's have a drink.

MOTHER: Better close the door.

CUT TO: INT. RALSTON BUILDING. DAY

High angle looking down. Some dealers are just leaving as JANE *comes in. It seems very dark in the building and the music which has been playing through the previous scene takes on a slightly menacing quality.* JANE *begins photographing and has her back to the camera as it begins to crane down from its high position to just behind her. She turns, as if aware of something and the camera cranes up, back to its high position. In the following cross-cut sequence the music does much of the linking.*

INT. HOSPITAL ROOM

NICK'S MOTHER *is holding a cigarette. The ash is long and she never actually smokes it. In her other hand is a small glass of whiskey.*

MOTHER: Have you ever had morphine?

NICK: No. What's it like?

MOTHER: Well . . . you have no idea of time. Sometimes I'm a little girl . . . I see my father . . . my mother . . . I talk with them. Sometimes I think I'm dead already. The first day you came was like that . . . when I was still in the other room. You came in with the nurse . . .

INT. RALSTON BUILDING

At first the screen is black but then a camera move reveals JANE *from a high angle through some banisters at the top of the stairs.* NICK'S MOTHER'S *voice continues over this scene.*

MOTHER (*Voice-over*): . . . you didn't recognize me of course . . . but I knew it was you . . . (JANE *moves to the foot of the stairs and begins to climb.*) . . . she pointed at my body.

INT. HOSPITAL

NICK *stares intently at his* MOTHER.

MOTHER: . . . sometimes I'm with your father. (*She drinks the Scotch.*)

NICK: What was my father like? (*There is a knock at the door.* NICK *hastily finishes his drink as the* NURSE *comes in.*)
NURSE: Mrs Anderson . . . (*She notices the drink and cigarettes.*) I think Dr Parker will have something to say about this.

INT. RALSTON BUILDING

A bright red glass vase, bathed in light, dominates the screen. Behind it, in the gloom, we see JANE *walking towards camera. Suddenly she hits light . . .*

EXT. HOSPITAL

NICK *runs down the steps to the taxi rank. A man stands next to a taxi reading a German newspaper.*
NICK: Can I get a ride back into town? (*The man lowers his paper and nods at* NICK.) Are you the driver? (*The man thinks carefully before speaking.*)
MAN: I . . . don't . . . speak English.
NICK: All right . . . forget it . . . thanks.
MAN: Goodbye.

INT. RALSTON BUILDING. MUSIC ROOM

Through a half-open door we see the silver metal phonograph that was in the opening sequence. It is on the desk. JANE *crosses frame from right to left. She looks down at the floor.*

ANGLE

On the floor we see broken pieces of 78 records.

ANGLE

She walks to the desk and picks up a record sleeve, blows the dust off it. The dust hangs in the air like a ghost. On the record sleeve is written 'Ralston'. She puts down the sleeve and opens the lid of the phonograph. There is a record on the turntable, covered in a fine layer of dust. JANE *wipes it off the label to read the title. It is upside down so she turns the record to read it. The needle is on the record and the movement of the record causes the turntable to start spinning. As it does so we see . . .*

FLASH IMAGE: *The two lovers from the opening sequence lying on the floor covered in blood. The record gets up to speed and we hear*

35

that it is the music from the opening sequence. Liebestraum *by Earl Bostic.*

ANGLE. JANE

She closes her eyes and listens to the music. Tears run down her cheeks. The camera begins a slow move in on her.

FLASH IMAGE: *The lovers*

ANGLE. *The record spinning*

ANGLE. JANE

From the darkness behind her a hand comes on to her shoulder. She opens her eyes but is not frightened. She turns and we see that it is NICK. *After a moment she takes the needle off the record.*

NICK: I was looking for you . . . are you all right? (JANE *looks at him.*)

JANE: Let's get back downstairs.

CUT TO: INT. RALSTON BUILDING. MAIN SPACE

MONTAGE OF DESTRUCTION. NICK *and* JANE, *both wearing face masks, photograph the destruction of the store. The noise is deafening. Workmen with sledgehammers smash the fittings whilst others carry out objects. The air is filled with dust. Sequence ends with a close up of* NICK *watching the carnage.*

EXT. RALSTON BUILDING

The black stretch Cadillac drives off revealing a group of old people watching the building.

INT. RALSTON BUILDING. LATE AFTERNOON

Everything is quiet now. NICK *and* JANE *sit by the window where they kissed the day before. She is cleaning her cameras with an air spray.*

NICK: What are you going to do now?

JANE: Go home and develop these films.

NICK: Will you have a drink with me . . . first? (JANE *concentrates hard on cleaning a lens and then looks up at him.*)

JANE: I don't think that's such a good idea.

NICK: Why?

JANE: We both know why . . . (*She carries on cleaning the cameras.*) . . . I should go home . . . take a shower . . .
NICK: Use mine. (JANE *concentrates hard on what she is doing and speaks very softly.*)
JANE: All right. (*She looks at him for a long time.*)

CUT TO: INT. HOTEL LOBBY

The desk clerk stares at NICK *and* JANE *who are waiting for the lift. Both of them look very dirty. Behind them an electrician is working on some exposed wiring. The lift arrives and they get in.*

INT. BEDROOM

We see the torn photograph on the wall. JANE *walks around to look at it. The bathroom door opens and* NICK *comes out, a towel around his neck, his hair wet.*
JANE: Is that your mother?
NICK: Yeah.
JANE: She was very beautiful.
NICK: Yes . . . she was.
JANE: Who's the man?
NICK: I dunno . . . my father, I guess. (JANE *goes into the bathroom and* NICK *stares at the photograph.*)

ANGLE

JANE *in the shower.*

ANGLE

NICK *lying on the bed. The phone rings and he looks at his watch, not expecting a call.*

ANGLE

JANE *towelling her hair by the mirror. She reacts to the sound of the phone.*

ANGLE

NICK *picks up the phone.*
NICK: Hello . . . (ANGLE. JANE *by the mirror.*) . . . hey Paul
. . . (ANGLE. NICK) . . . she left about twenty minutes ago. She said she had to pick up some dry cleaning or something so she should be on her way home . . . bye. (NICK *puts the phone down and curses. He gets off the bed.* ANGLE. JANE *listens. Through the door.*) Jane?

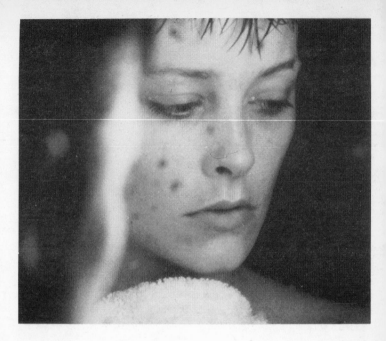

JANE: Yes.

NICK: I left something in the building. I'll see you down there, OK?

JANE: OK . . . I'll meet you there. (*She looks at herself in the mirror*).

INT. RALSTON BUILDING LOBBY

NICK *slams his keys down on to a glass counter and swears. He walks up to a group of mannequins and shoves them hard, knocking them over.*

NICK: Shit . . . fuck.

INT. RESTAURANT. NIGHT

NICK *and* JANE *face each other in a booth. The place is quite full and noisy. They are both drinking beer.* JANE *is smoking.*

NICK: This isn't right. I pushed it. I'm sorry.

JANE: Don't be sorry . . . so what are we going to do?

NICK: Nothing I guess. It's just that I . . . (*He touches her hand.*)

JANE: I really like you too. (*They hold hands.*)

NICK: OK.

JANE: Let's go. I want to show you something.

INT. HOSPITAL. NIGHT

A needle is pushed into an arm. We see the NIGHT NURSE.

NIGHT NURSE: There. That should make you feel better, Mrs
   Anderson.

ANGLE. NICK'S MOTHER.

MOTHER: Stay with me a while.

NIGHT NURSE: What's the matter?

MOTHER: I'm frightened.
   (*It is now possible to see that the same actress who played*
   CINDY *in the whorehouse is also playing* NIGHT NURSE. *The
   same is true of the other whores, they are also the other nurses.*)

EXT. STREET. NIGHT

JANE'*s pick-up pulls up outside a large Victorian mansion which is
floodlit.*

JANE: I thought this might interest you. It was built by the
   same architect who designed the store.

NICK: I like the store better. Who lives there?

JANE: The last surviving Ralston. Barnett Ralston the . . .
   fourth. (*Someone comes out of the house. The black stretch
   limo is parked by the door, the chauffeur waiting.*) That's him.
   (*She turns off the engine and the headlights.* RALSTON *stops to
   light a cigarette before getting into his car.*)

NICK: What happened to the rest of the family?

JANE: You don't know . . . about the murders? That's why the
   store was closed down. His mother was having an affair
   with an employee. They used to meet at the store, very late
   at night . . . and his father found out. (*The limo drives out
   of the entrance and exits.*) . . . and he caught them one night
   . . . and he shot them . . . and then he killed himself. The
   next day, when the police found the bodies they discovered
   that she was still alive. She'd been shot in the head. She
   was brain dead, but still alive. (NICK *strokes the back of*
   JANE'*s head.*) The Ralston Memorial Hospital was opened
   the following year.

NICK: She must be dead by now.

JANE: Yes, she must be. (JANE *closes her eyes as* NICK *continues stroking her.*)
NICK: Jane . . . (*She turns to him and they kiss.*)

CUT TO: INT. HOSPITAL. NIGHT

NICK'S MOTHER *is almost asleep but her lips move feverishly. She is very disturbed.*
MOTHER: I wouldn't have hurt him . . . please don't . . . don't take him away from me . . .
NIGHT NURSE: No one is going to take him away . . . shhh.
(*The* NURSE *strokes her hand gently.*)

CUT TO: EXT. HOTEL. NIGHT

The pick-up drives off and NICK *walks over to the hotel entrance. The door is locked and the night porter is asleep, his leg in a cast.* NICK *curses as he remembers leaving his keys in the Ralston Building.*

INT. RALSTON BUILDING

At first it is black and then we hear the door opening and a shaft of light reveals the keys on the glass counter where NICK *left them.* NICK *picks them up and the camera moves up to his face just as he hears something. It is the sound of a woman.*

ANGLE

NICK *on the stairs, listening. He begins to climb.*

ANGLE

NICK *in the Music Department. He shines a flashlight around. We hear the sound of piano strings and he shines his flashlight on to one of the grand pianos.* NICK *walks towards the piano and takes a step up on to a little stage. He looks into the open lid of the piano and there is a tremendous noise as a cat jumps out leaving a dead rat behind.* NICK *gets a huge fright.*

ANGLE

NICK *comes down the foot of the stairs into a group of mannequins.*
NICK: Fucking cat . . . scared the living shit out of me. (*He walks through the mannequins and again he hears something. He looks around but everything is still. He carries on, but frightened now. Suddenly we see a figure move quickly behind a*

mannequin. NICK *looks at the space and slowly* BARNETT RALSTON *appears.*)

RALSTON: Munsen? (*He begins to walk towards* NICK *who runs through the mannequins, knocking them over. He trips and falls, striking his head against the edge of a counter.* RALSTON's *face fills the screen as he looks down at* NICK.) Munsen . . . you're dead.

DISSOLVE TO: INT. JANE'S DARKROOM

In the red safety light we see JANE *in her bra and pants working on her photographs. She pulls a print out of a tray and holds it up to inspect it. We see that it is a photograph of* NICK.

DISSOLVE TO: INT. RALSTON BUILDING. DAWN

NICK *lying in a pool of blood in the grey dawn light coming from the open door. The camera is above him and moves down as he wakes and touches his head.*

CUT TO: BLACK

TITLE. THURSDAY
In black we hear very loud noises of destruction and then as the picture fades in we see the feet of workmen as they go about the business of demolition in the building. We see a pair of high-heeled shoes and the camera pans up to reveal JANE *as she comes into the building looking for* NICK. *She covers her ears to block out the din and walks carefully over splintered wood and debris. She looks up the stairs and sees* NICK *as he comes down. He has a band-aid on his forehead. They stand close together at the foot of the stairs.*
JANE: Hi.
NICK: Hi.
JANE: I'm late . . . sorry.
NICK: It's all right. (*She sees the cut on his head.*)
JANE: What happened to you?
NICK: I fell.
JANE: It looks pretty dirty . . .
NICK: Can we get out of here?

CUT TO: EXT. PAUL AND JANE'S HOUSE. DAY

JANE's *pick-up pulls up outside her house.*

41

INT. HOUSE

A maid is cleaning the hall as NICK *and* JANE *come in.* JANE *is surprised.*

MAID: Hi, Mrs Kessler.

JANE: Maria . . . what are you doing here?

MAID: I always come on Thursdays, Mrs Kessler.

JANE: Oh . . . right . . . OK. (NICK *and* JANE *exit.*)

INT. DARKROOM. DAY

NICK *looks at the photograph of himself that* JANE *has pinned up on the wall along with the pictures of the building. He is very serious. He is hardly recognizable as the same person from three days earlier.* JANE *is cleaning the cut on his head.*

NICK: The guy that was killed in the building, not Ralston, the other guy, what was his name?

JANE: His name was Munsen. (NICK *looks up at her. She has her hands on his head. He slides her skirt up and touches her. She drops the cotton swab that she was holding and holds her skirt as he puts his hand between her legs. She moves back to the wall where the pictures are.*) Don't do that. (NICK *stands and walks to her. He touches her breasts and she covers his hands with hers. As they kiss . . .*)

ANGLE

The MAID *passes the open door and sees them. She turns away.*
JANE *moves away from* NICK.
MAID: Shall I do the bathroom now, Mrs Kessler?

CUT TO: INT. HOSPITAL ROOM. DAY

NICK'S MOTHER *is bright and cheerful as a young nurse fusses
around her bed straightening the sheets.*
MOTHER: What's the time, nurse?
NURSE: Your son will be here soon, Mrs Anderson.

EXT. HOSPITAL

JANE'S *pick-up comes around the corner.*

INT. HOSPITAL

NURSE: Here . . . I've brought you a newspaper to read. (*The*
    NURSE *gives* NICK'S MOTHER *a local paper to look at.*)

EXT. HOSPITAL

NICK *kissing* JANE *passionately through the window of the pick-up.*

INT. HOSPITAL

*We see a blurred image that comes into focus as the Ralston
Building. It is the front page of the newspaper.*
MOTHER: Nurse, what town are we in? What's the name of this
    town? (*The* NURSE *is worried by the tone of her voice and
    answers cautiously.*)
NURSE: Why, surely you know Mrs Anderson, we're in
    Elderstown of course.

ANGLE

MOTHER *makes a huge effort to get out of bed, finding reserves of
strength that should have been long exhausted.*
NURSE: Oh . . . don't get out of bed, Mrs Anderson. (*She tries
    to stop her but cannot. She shouts.*) Sister!

INT. HOSPITAL CORRIDOR

As NICK *steps out of the lift he hears a frail scream. He stops and listens . . .*

ANGLE

The door opens and the SISTER *runs in to help the* NURSE. NICK'S MOTHER *is out of control, screaming and crying as she tries to escape from the bed.* NICK *comes into the room and sees all this. He is very upset. The* SISTER *eases him out of the room.*
SISTER: I think it would be better if you waited outside, Mr
    Kaminsky.

CUT TO: INT. DR PARKER'S OFFICE

NICK, *alone in the office waiting for* DR PARKER. *He sees his mother's file on the desk and he picks it up and begins looking through it.*

TEXT

Widespread cancer . . . further surgery not advisable . . . fourth term in mental institute . . . treatment for depression . . .

NICK *skips lots of pages and arrives near the front of the file.*

TEXT

Patient wishes to revert to maiden name of Anderson.

ANGLE. NICK'S FACE

NICK *is very puzzled by this. He slowly turns the page one nearer to the front of the file.*

CLOSE UP ON THE PAGE

On the top of the page is his mother's married name.

TEXT

MUNSEN, LILLIAN (MRS)

EXTREME CLOSE UP *of* NICK's *eyes as he absorbs this information.*

CUT TO: INT. POLICE STATION. FILE ROOM

SHERIFF RICKER *leads* NICK *around the room. Shelves are stuffed with old files. Ahead of them is a clerk.*

RICKER: If anybody can find this, Matt can.

MATT: Ralston . . . Ralston . . . Ralston . . . it's around here some place. (MATT *climbs a ladder and we see his face in* CLOSE UP *framed by files as he looks for it.*) I remember the case well. I was just a rookie at the time. I was the first cop on the scene . . . lotta blood, whole lotta blood. Guys pecker was still up like a pole . . . good-looking broad . . . what a waste, took the lab boys forever to get there . . . and I was staring at her and . . . noticed this little vein in her neck was still kind of . . . throbbing . . .

ANGLE

NICK *lost in thought below as* RICKER *leers at him.*

MATT: Ah . . . here it is. (*He hands the file down to* RICKER *who hesitates before handing it over to* NICK. NICK *walks away with the file.*)

RICKER: Nick . . . (NICK *turns.*) They seem like a real happy couple.

CUT TO: EXT. MAIN STREET. LATE AFTERNOON

NICK *is walking quickly down the street. He is very agitated and breaks into a run. He is carrying the file.*

CUT TO: INT. HOTEL ROOM

The door opens and NICK *comes in but then stops short.*

NICK'S POINT OF VIEW

The room has been gutted. All his things have gone. The furniture has gone. The floorboards have been ripped up. Bared cable can be seen. We hear the sound of the DESK CLERK *approaching.*

CLERK: Ah . . . Mr Kaminsky . . . The electricians had a change of plan, Mr Kaminsky, and they needed to get to the wiring in your room. We've moved all your things into the adjoining room. It's exactly the same size.

NICK: The room where the couple were staying? (*The* CLERK *looks puzzled.*)

CLERK: There's nobody else on this floor, Mr Kaminsky, just you . . . all week. This way please. (*The* CLERK *walks off leaving* NICK *in a state of complete confusion. On the soundtrack we hear the slow piano blues which plays through the next sequence.*)

CUT TO: NEW HOTEL ROOM

The door closes and NICK *looks around. The room is a mirror image of the other room. Everything is the opposite position to before. Everything has been carefully laid out in its opposite position. Even the photograph of his mother has been pinned on to the wall.*

ANGLE

NICK *sits on the bed and puts the box file next to him. He opens his filofax and looks up a number which he then dials. It takes a while to connect and he opens the file and starts to take out the contents one by one. We hear the ringing tone through the receiver.*

ANGLE

We see ballistics reports, autopsy reports, coroner's reports. The ringing stops and we hear the characteristic sound of a recorded message. It is JANE's *voice. As he listens,* NICK *pulls out a brown photographic envelope. He opens the flap and takes out a pile of ten by eight photographs.*

JANE (*Voice-over*): Hi, neither Paul nor Jane Kessler is in right now but if you leave your name and number, we'll get back to you as soon as we can. Thanks for calling . . . please speak after you hear the tone.

(*The pictures show the office in the Ralston Building as it was after the murder. The three bodies are on the floor.* BARNETT *is slumped near the door. His wife is near the desk, her white dress up past her waist.* MUNSEN *is near her.*)

ANGLE

We hear the tone on the phone but NICK *doesn't leave a message, he just stares at the picture.*

CLOSE UP OF THE PICTURE

We zoom in slowly on the black and white photograph, homing in on the face of PETER MUNSEN. *It is* NICK. MUNSEN *and* NICK *are so alike it is like looking at the same person.* NICK *covers his face with his hands.*

DISSOLVE TO: INT. HOTEL ROOM. MIDDLE OF THE NIGHT

High angle shot of NICK *asleep on top of the bed. He is still fully clothed. All around the bed are the contents of the police file. The photographs.*

DISSOLVE TO: EXT. RALSTON MANSION. MORNING

NICK *gets out of a yellow cab.*

ANGLE

NICK *walks up the steps of the mansion and the front door opens as he gets there. The* CHAUFFEUR *asks him in.* NICK *is wearing a dark suit, white shirt and tie and seems to have pulled himself together again.*

INT. MANSION

Looking down the stairs we see NICK *and the* CHAUFFEUR *come into the hallway.*

CHAUFFEUR: Mr Ralston would like to know the name of the newspaper that you work for.

NICK: It's not a newspaper . . . it's a quarterly magazine . . . on architecture. Here's my card. (*The* CHAUFFEUR *takes the card and goes upstairs, looking at it.*)

CHAUFFEUR: He'll be down shortly.

ANGLE

NICK *walks down the hallway and looks into a red room. Very faintly on the soundtrack we hear* Liebestraum. NICK *listens and then walks on.*

47

ANGLE

NICK *opens a mirrored door which reveals a dark passageway. The music is louder. He walks into the passage and another set of doors opens in front of him.*

ANGLE

NICK *looks at a ballroom. Strong white light coming in from the many-curtained windows. On the far side of the room is* JANE *who is sitting in a chair next to a small table. She is crying, her head in her hands. On the table is the metal phonograph from which the music is coming.* NICK *walks towards her.*
NICK: What's the matter, Jane?

ANGLE

In another part of the room an empty wheelchair spins around.

ANGLE

JANE *looks up at* NICK. *She has blood on her hands and a wound on her forehead.*
JANE: Help me . . . please . . .

IMAGE: NICK *running through the mannequins.*

INT. HOTEL ROOM. NIGHT

NICK *sits up in bed screaming. The phone is ringing by the bed but then it stops. He is drenched with sweat. He puts his hands to his head. His cut is bleeding.*

CUT TO BLACK

TITLE: FRIDAY

INT. DR PARKER'S OFFICE. DAY

DR PARKER *is seated behind his desk, talking to* NICK.
DR PARKER: What do you want us to do, Nick? Your mother is
    slipping away from us. Now . . . we can keep her alive for
    quite a long time. It's an expensive process. I'd like you to
    think about it.
NICK: May I see her?
DR PARKER: As soon as she regains consciousness, we'll call you

48

CUT TO: INT. RALSTON BUILDING. DAY

BUDDY *and two of his workmen are blocking the entrance as* NICK *comes in. They seem quite sinister.*

NICK: Hi.

BUDDY: Hey . . . how're you doing? Say . . . you about finished in here now? It's going to be getting dangerous . . . I'd appreciate it if you'd keep away now.

NICK: Paul told me that if I . . .

BUDDY: I just spoken with Mr Kessler. I have his OK on this. (*The men stare at each other for some moments.*)

CUT TO: INT. BEDROOM. HOTEL. AFTERNOON

NICK *is sitting on the bed, looking out of the window. On the sound track we hear the slow piano blues with some clarinet. There is a gentle knock on the door.* NICK *gets up and opens the door. It is* JANE. *They are shy with each other.*

JANE: Hello . . .

NICK: Hi. (JANE *smiles nervously.* NICK *gently pulls her into the room.*)

MONTAGE: *They lie down on the bed and begin to make love, undressing each other.*

FLASH IMAGE: NICK'S MOTHER *writhing around, her face contorted with anguish.*

ANGLE

JANE *takes* NICK'S *hand and puts it between her legs. He begins to arouse her. The camera begins to track along them towards the wall.*

JANE: Fuck me. (*The camera reaches the wall and starts to go into a black area. As it does so the phone begins to ring. The camera goes through the wall and into the wrecked room where* NICK *was before. We hear them through the wall . . .*)

NICK: I've got to get it . . . it could be the hospital . . . Hello . . . this is Mr Kaminsky . . . (*The camera comes back through the wall and into the bedroom.* NICK *is sitting up on the bed talking on the phone.* JANE *is twined around him, still making love to him.*) Un huh . . . I'll be there as soon as I can, Dr Parker. (*He puts the phone down.* JANE *kisses his back and tries to pull him down on the bed.*)

49

CUT TO: INT. PICK-UP. AFTEROON

JANE *drives.* NICK *watches her. They are both still very aroused.*
NICK: Will you come in with me?
JANE: If you want me to. (NICK *plays with her hair and touches*
her breast.) I'll crash if you do that.

CUT TO: INT. HOSPITAL CORRIDOR

NICK *and* JANE *come out of the lift and* NICK *walks ahead towards*
his MOTHER*'s door. He stops and as* JANE *catches up he kisses her*
passionately. A nurse passes and goes into a room. They part.
JANE: Go on. (NICK *walks reluctantly to his* MOTHER*'s room,*
opens the door and goes in. JANE *looks around the deserted*
corridor and sits down opposite the lift. There is the sound of a
distant storm. Thunder rumbling.

INT. MOTHER'S ROOM

High camera angle looking down. NICK'S MOTHER *is in bed, very*
still. Seated by the bed is a young nurse reading a magazine. NICK
is standing at the foot of the bed.
NURSE: Mrs Anderson . . . your son is here. (NICK *sits down in*
the other chair by the bed.)

INT. CORRIDOR

CLOSE UP *of* JANE *sitting, leaning against the wall. Her eyes are*
closed. She is humming quietly to herself. The camera angle widens
revealing the corridor behind her. Two ORDERLIES *are pushing a*
wheelchair down the corridor towards JANE. *It is not possible to see*
whether the figure in the wheelchair is a man or a woman. One of
the wheels gives off a squeek as it rubs against something. The score
starts to increase the tension. The thunder is a little closer. The
ORDERLIES *arrive at the lift with the wheelchair. One of them*
presses the button but the light does not come on.
FIRST ORDERLY: Shit . . . someone left that door open again.
Wait here, I'll go and fix it. (JANE *watches, amused, as he*
goes off leaving the other ORDERLY *alone with the figure in the*
wheelchair. The corridor is very gloomy and it is not possible to
make out anything but a silhouette.)

INT. MOTHER'S ROOM

NICK'S MOTHER *tries to speak but has great difficulty. The nurse reads her magazine.*

EXT. CORRIDOR

The remaining ORDERLY *waits. Down the corridor a door opens and the* SISTER *appears. She sees the* ORDERLY.

SISTER: Ben . . . would you come here for a moment?

ORDERLY: I'm waiting for Jack . . . this elevator's stuck . . .

SISTER: This will only take a moment.

ORDERLY: I'm supposed to wait here with her, you know.

SISTER: Ben!

ORDERLY: OK. (*The* SISTER *goes back in and the* ORDERLY *leans down to talk to the woman in the wheelchair.*) Ma'am . . . I'll just be a sec . . . OK? (*He goes off leaving* JANE *alone with the woman.*)

INT. MOTHER'S ROOM

NICK'S MOTHER *tries to speak again and succeeds in making a small but unintelligible sound. The nurse turns a page of her magazine.*

INT. CORRIDOR

The lift doors open just in front of the wheelchair.

INT. MOTHER'S ROOM

CLOSE ANGLE *on* NICK'S *face. His* MOTHER'S *hand comes slowly up into frame. She opens her hand, inviting him to hold it.*

INT. CORRIDOR

JANE *looks worriedly at the woman in the wheelchair. She looks down the corridor but it is empty.*

ANGLE

CLOSE UP *of the wheel of the wheelchair. A lifeless hand falls into frame. It twitches.*

INT. MOTHER'S ROOM

NICK *stares at his* MOTHER's *hand. He hesitates and then brings his hand to hers. She grasps it.* NICK *is very nervous.*

INT. CORRIDOR

The hand tries to push the wheelchair towards the open lift. JANE *watches, worried.*
JANE: Ma'am? (JANE *gets up and goes to help the woman.*) Ma'am
. . . I think you should wait for the nurse . . . ma'am?

ANGLE. JANE'S POINT OF VIEW

The woman slowly brings her head up and we see that she has a large indentation on her forehead, a bullet wound scar. JANE *is very frightened. She backs off in horror as the sightless eyes of the woman look from left to right.*

ANGLE

JANE *backs towards* NICK'S MOTHER's *room.*

INT. MOTHER'S ROOM

NICK's *hand is slowly brought towards his* MOTHER's *face.*

INT. CORRIDOR

JANE *edges backwards, away from the woman in the wheelchair, towards* NICK'S MOTHER's *room.*

INT. MOTHER'S ROOM

NICK'S MOTHER *kisses his hand.*

INT. CORRIDOR

JANE *opens the door and goes in as* . . .

INT. MOTHER'S ROOM

NICK'S MOTHER *looks at him strangely.*
MOTHER: I can smell her on you. (*The door closes and they both*

look at JANE *as she comes in, horrified by what she has already seen.*)

NICK: Jane? What's the matter?

ANGLE

NICK'S MOTHER *makes a huge effort and tries to climb out of bed to get at* JANE. *She is like an animal. In slow motion we see the nurses trying to restrain her and the orderlies coming into the room to help.* JANE *is in shock and edges out of the door as* NICK'S MOTHER *is dragged back into the bed.*

INT. CORRIDOR

The next sequence is hand held and all in one take.
JANE *runs out of the room and is again confronted by the woman in the wheelchair. The lift doors close.* JANE *stops and looks at her. There is pathos in this moment. The camera wheels around her in a half circle momentarily revealing two men walking down the corridor towards her.* JANE *hesitates for a moment. She is crying. Then she walks down the corridor passing the two men who are* DR PARKER *and* BARNETT RALSTON. *As she passes them,* DR PARKER *recognizes her.*

DR PARKER: Jane . . . why how very nice . . . (JANE *walks down the corridor and out of sight as* RALSTON *goes to the woman in the wheelchair and kneels by her. In the background we see* NICK *running out of his* MOTHER'S *room.*)

NICK: Jane . . . (*He stops short when he sees* RALSTON *who looks at him for a moment before turning back to the woman in the wheelchair. He holds her hands.*)

RALSTON: Hello, Mother.

CUT TO: EXT. STREET. NIGHT

Rain is falling heavily on the street. Thunder is heard. A jeep drives into shot and BUDDY *goes to the window of the car whose window winds down and reveals* PAUL.

PAUL: Hey Buddy . . . How's it going?

BUDDY: We're a little behind, but we'll make it. I wasn't expecting you 'til tonight.

PAUL: I got the early flight. You seen Jane?

BUDDY: Not since this morning.

PAUL: OK . . . I'll check back with you later. (*The jeep drives out of shot.*)

CUT TO: INT. HOSPITAL. NIGHT

NICK'S MOTHER *is in a coma, watched by the* NIGHT NURSE. *A drip-feed can be seen in the background.*

CUT TO: INT. HOTEL ROOM

NICK *sits in the window watching the rain. He is smoking a cigarette.*

ANGLE

The photograph of his MOTHER *on the wall.*

ANGLE

Closer shot of NICK. *He notices something on the street below.*

EXT. STREET

The rain is torrential as NICK *crosses the street. He is not wearing a coat. A young man with his girlfriend stops* NICK *and says something to him. It's as if he knows* NICK. NICK *walks on towards the Ralston Building.*

ANGLE

CLOSE SHOT *of the first floor window of the music room office.*

CUT TO: INT. MUSIC ROOM

NICK *walks into the wrecked and empty music department and stops. In the following sequence the use of colour indicates present time, the use of black and white indicates a flashback to the time of the opening scene.*

ANGLE

In the office we see JANE *in silhouette. She is waiting for* NICK *who walks into the shot and goes to her. She is leaning against the desk. He takes her coat off. She stands and kisses him then pulls up her dress and takes off her pants. He pulls her down to the floor.*

IMAGE. BLACK AND WHITE: *High-heeled shoes spinning. We saw this in the opening sequence of the film.*

54

EXT. BUILDING

PAUL's *jeep pulls up in the rain and he gets out and walks towards the building.*

IMAGE. BLACK AND WHITE: *The* WOMAN IN WHITE, *spinning.*

INT. OFFICE

NICK *and* JANE *making love on the floor. She is sitting on him.*

IMAGE. BLACK AND WHITE: *The* MAN IN THE HAT *coming into the rear entrance of the building. In the background is the period Cadillac. It is raining.*

INT. HOSPITAL

NICK'S MOTHER. *She is agitated. Her head moves from side to side. She is upside down in the frame.*

INT. OFFICE

NICK *and* JANE *making love. They are both very aroused.*

INT. HOSPITAL

NICK'S MOTHER *agitated. Her eyes open and look straight into the camera.*

IMAGE. BLACK AND WHITE: *The* MAN IN THE HAT *walking up the stairs.*

INT. MUSIC DEPARTMENT

We see a hand holding a gun. The camera tilts up to the face and we see it is PAUL. *He looks into the office. We can hear the sound of the lovers.*

INT. OFFICE

NICK *and* JANE *making love.*
JANE: Oh . . . come in me.

NICK: Tell me that you love me. Say it . . . say it . . .
JANE: I love you.

INT. HOSPITAL

NICK'S MOTHER's *body arches up, her head goes back and her mouth opens as she tries to scream.*

SEQUENCE. BLACK AND WHITE: *The door to the office opens and we see the lovers from the opening sequence making love against the desk . . . The screen is black but then we see the rounded stomach of a pregnant woman crossing frame from left to right . . . We see the lovers reflected in the glass that covers the photograph of the Ralston Building . . . In* CLOSE UP *we see a woman's face as she comes out of the shadows. Her cheeks are wet with tears. The sound of the lovers is very strong. It is the woman in* NICK'S *photograph – his* MOTHER *as a young woman . . . We see the lovers clearly and although they are in the period clothes of the 1950s we see that it is* NICK *and* JANE *. . . The* YOUNG MOTHER *points a gun . . . The lovers are like animals with each other . . . The* YOUNG MOTHER *fires the gun . . . All of the sound goes from the soundtrack . . . The* WOMAN IN WHITE *mouths a scream as her lover is hit.*

INT. HOSPITAL. COLOUR. PRESENT TIME

NICK'S MOTHER *mouths a silent scream.*

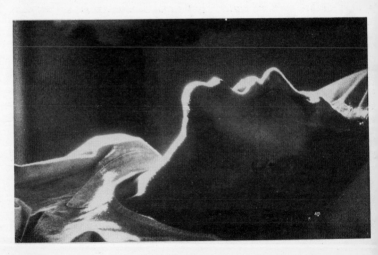

BLACK AND WHITE SEQUENCE (*cont'd*): *Fast* ZOOM IN *on the* WOMAN IN WHITE *as . . . The* YOUNG MOTHER *fires again.*

INT. HOSPITAL. COLOUR. PRESENT TIME

NICK'S MOTHER *reacts again.*

BLACK AND WHITE SEQUENCE (*cont'd*): *The* YOUNG MOTHER *fires again and . . .* THE MAN IN THE HAT *clutches his stomach as he is shot.*

INT. OFFICE. PRESENT DAY. COLOUR

JANE's *head goes back as she and* NICK *climax.*

INT. HOSPITAL. PRESENT TIME

NICK'S MOTHER, *her body still arched, starts to slip back down.*

INT. OFFICE. PRESENT TIME

JANE *slowly brings her head down to* NICK. *She passes through bars of light and it seems as if she is falling.*

INT. HOSPITAL. PRESENT TIME

NICK'S MOTHER's *head comes to rest on the pillow and the tension goes out of her body. The* NURSE *stares at her for a moment and then reaches over and closes her eyes and then makes the sign of the cross. As she does so the sound fades back in and we hear the thunder which is abating.*

INT. MUSIC DEPARTMENT. PRESENT TIME

PAUL *stares into the office. He is crying. There is no sound of the lovers.*

INT. OFFICE. PRESENT TIME

High angle of NICK *and* JANE. *They are lying together on the floor, completely still, their arms and legs wrapped around each other. On the soundtrack we hear the opening to the piano version of* Liebestraum.

INT. MUSIC DEPARTMENT. PRESENT TIME

PAUL *turns and walks into the shadow.*

IMAGE: *A young girl sits at a piano and is playing the music that we can hear. It is the girl with the red hair that we saw in* NICK's *first dream. She is positioned to the left of frame and the rest of the frame is black. In this black space the end credits begin to roll and continue to do so until the end of the piece of music.*